Travels in the

ORIENT

In Marco Polo's Footsteps

An eternal caravan along the Silk Route.

Konecky & Konecky
150 Fifth Ave.
New York, NY 10011

This edition published by special arrangement with Vilo Diffusion
Copyright © 1997 Vilo
All rights reserved
ISBN: 1-56852-238-X
Printed and bound in Spain

TEXTS AND PHOTOGRAPHS
ALAIN CHENEVIERE

Travels in the

ORIENT

In Marco Polo's Footsteps

EDITOR IN CHIEF
ROGER SABATER

TRANSLATED BY
LENORE RIGUET

KONECKY&KONECKY

From the banks of the Ganges to the steppes of central Asia,
buildings and monuments of unequaled grandeur
mark the old caravan routes.

Introduction

Almost seven hundred years ago *Description of the World* was published; it was an exceptional book which told of the adventures of a Venetian named Marco Polo. Whether it was known as *Il Milione*, *the Book of Marvels* or *The Travels of Marco Polo*, it was to become a bible for all travelers and was to make its author one of the most famous people on earth.

"Lords, emperors and kings, dukes and marquises, counts, knights and townsfolk, and all of you who wish to know the different races of mankind and the peculiarities of the different regions of the world and to learn of their customs, take this book and have it read to you. It will tell them to you in plain and due order, as they were related by Messer Marco Polo, a wise and noble citizen of Venice, who has seen them with his own eyes." That is how *Description of the World* begins.

We have taken this thirteenth century traveler at his word. We read his book and decided to make the same journey, to set out in his tracks and, to the extent that it was possible, to see for ourselves the landscapes and monuments that his eyes had seen, and to feel in our hearts the emotions that he had felt at the sight of so many different peoples. It was not an easy undertaking, for the regions he crossed have changed considerably since then. But we made his magnificent journey; not all at once, to be sure, that would have been impossible in our troubled twentieth century, but with great patience over the course of many trips to these fabulous lands and seas.

Certain photographs were taken over fifteen years ago; the most recent are less than six months old. Patiently, we reconstructed the route, his as well as ours, like a jigsaw puzzle on which one works night after night until slowly but surely it takes shape.

This album is as faithful a portrait as possible of the route the illustrious Venetian and his companions actually took. We followed exclusively the indications given in *Description of the World*. Certain episodes and places which Marco Polo could not have known had to be eliminated. As was the practice in the Middle Ages, at times he took liberties with the strict historical and geographical truth, or else he reported rumors that were widespread at the time. Most of his book, however, is extremely factual. Each time he did not personally see what he recorded, he took the precaution of indicating that "he had been told" or that "he had heard." It is no doubt his constant concern for the truth that underlies this splendid autobiographical work that has made *Description of the World* a best-seller throughout the centuries.

Table of contents

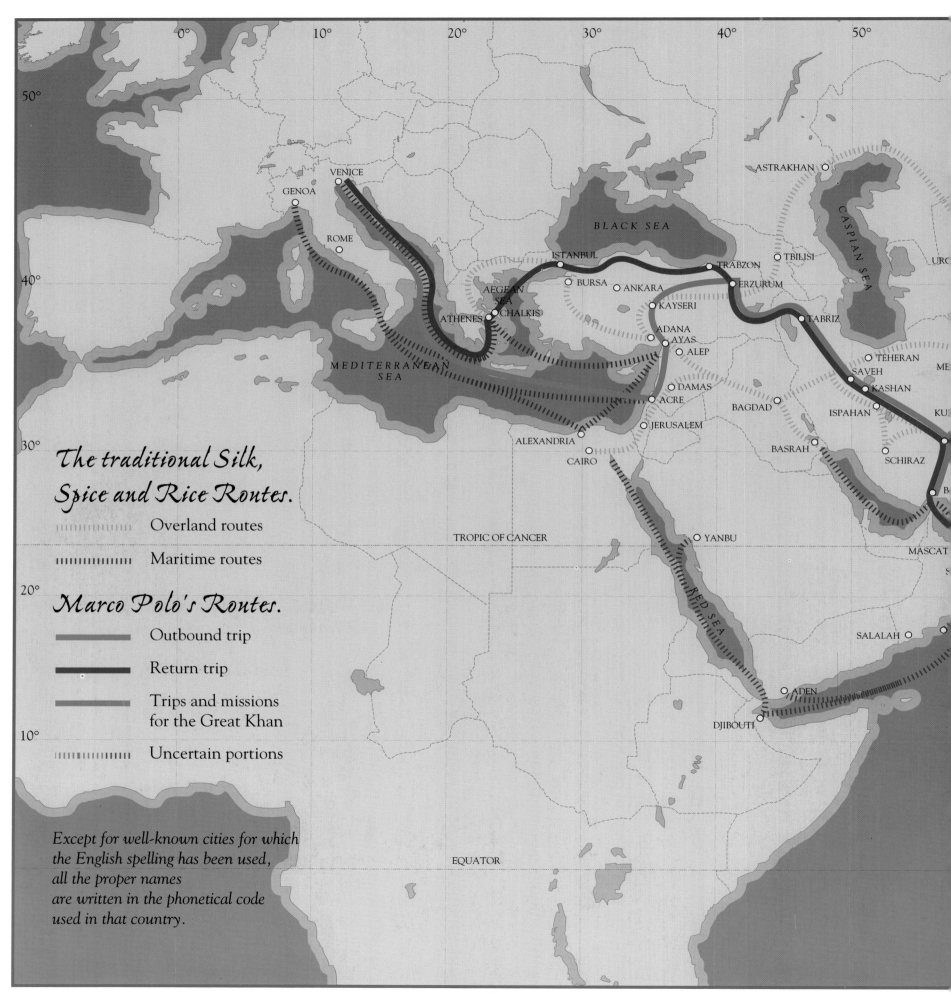

The traditional Silk,
Spice and Rice Routes.

|||||||||| Overland routes

|||||||||| Maritime routes

Marco Polo's Routes.

——— Outbound trip

——— Return trip

——— Trips and missions
for the Great Khan

|||||||||| Uncertain portions

*Except for well-known cities for which
the English spelling has been used,
all the proper names
are written in the phonetical code
used in that country.*

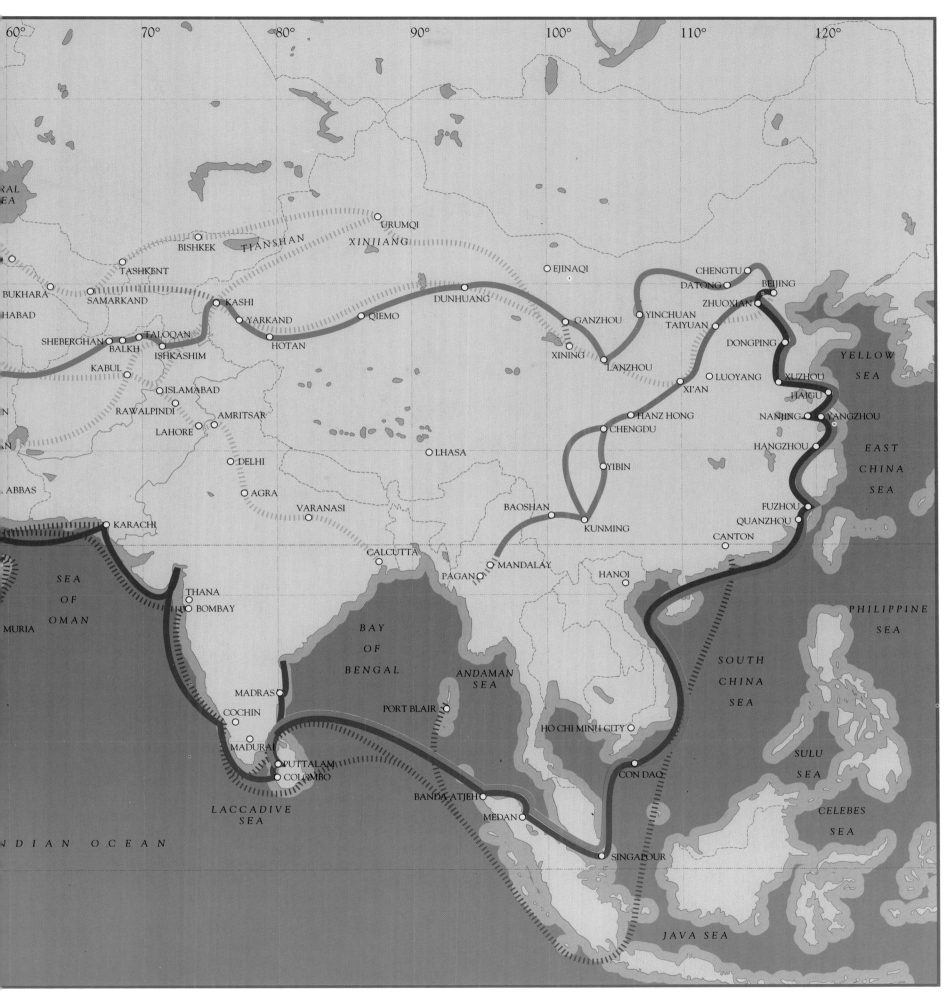

The Fabulous Story of the Silk Route

Silk was born in China.

Recent archeological excavations on neolithic sites in the Shanxi region have revealed silk cocoons,
although it is difficult to determine if they are natural cocoons or if they result from farming.
On the other hand, there is proof that approximately four thousand years ago, for the first time on earth,
man extracted threads from the cocoon of a Bombyx mori caterpillar,
a worm that subsists on mulberry (Morus alba) leaves.
Shortly thereafter, various texts mention the beginnings of silkworm breeding
in the central basins of the Yellow (Huanghe) and the Shandong Rivers.
However, the veritable beginnings of the silk industry and the marketing of silk
date from around the sixth century BC.
In Chinese mythology silk threads are derived from the hair of the sky god.
According to tradition, the origin of silk can be attributed to two women.
An ancient legend has it that the Empress Xi Lingshi was pursued by a serpent and found refuge in a mulberry tree.
There she discovered silkworm cocoons hanging from the branches.
Pulling on one of the threads that was protruding, she obtained mankind's first silk thread.
She later became the goddess of silk. Another myth tells of how Leizu, a concubine of the Emperor Huangdi,
who wanted "clothes as bright as divine finery," initiated mulberry growing and silkworm breeding.

The Silk, Spice and Rice Routes

As early as the second century,
the overland and maritime routes competed for East - West trade.

For nearly two thousand years before the Christian era,
trade relations existed between the Far East and the Middle East. Whereas trade in the Mediterranean occurred
on a very small scale as, slowly, century after century, the Phoenicians, the Hittites, the Minoans, the Greeks,
the Persians and the Egyptians learned to deal with each other despite their antagonisms,
in Asia exchanges were already highly developed, particularly between China and India.

CHINESE TRADING SUPREMACY

Goods followed the ancient caravan trails or were transported by boat across the China Sea. Foremost among the merchandise were silk, spices and rice.

The bulk of the Chinese trade was directed towards central Asia and India. There were two main routes possible to reach the former, one which passed through the Taklamakan Desert, the other to the south. They joined together in Persia. As silk generally took the northern route, while most of the spices were sent to the south, they came to be known, respectively, as the Silk Route and the Spice Route.

China and southern India, where the largest kingdoms were then located, did business principally by sea. As rice was the main commodity transported between the two countries, the maritime route naturally became the Rice Route.

Later on silk, spices and rice were transported by each route. Nevertheless, the original names prevailed until the third century A.D., when at first they were all called the Silk Routes and finally the Silk Route.

The relations the Chinese, or the "the Sons of the Sky," as they called themselves, maintained with Asian and Indian merchants, as well as, to a lesser degree, with the kingdoms of southern Arabia, had convinced them of the interest their products aroused, especially silk. They knew that far to the west lay rich countries that would, undoubtedly, like to trade with them. Therefore, they undertook to expand their Far Eastern trade network towards the west.

The first to do so were the Qins. In 221 B.C. Emperor Qin Shi Huangdi mounted the throne, giving his name to the country and its inhabitants. He founded a powerful, centralized state whose borders he protected by the imposing Great Wall of China. Once the stability of the empire was ensured, he began to develop trade relations with India. Then he turned to the west, where, it was said, there were powerful kingdoms. To reach them, however, it was first necessary to guarantee that caravans could safely cross central Asia. Thus, he opened the first major trade routes to the west, building and then enlarging the roads. Often dating back several centuries, the old caravan trails that linked together the different parts of China or brought China closer to the southern and western outer provinces, rapidly became major thoroughfares. By guaranteeing the safety, the maintenance and the development of these new roads, the Chinese monarchy stimulated the great march towards the west.

THE MARCH TOWARDS THE WEST

For four centuries, the next dynasty, the Hans, were to complete the work begun by the Qins. The Middle Empire, as the Chinese called it, believing their country to be the center of the world, turned outwards for most of its economic activities. To attain the far-off western markets, the Chinese sovereigns first brought into subjection the kingdoms of central Asia. In 30 B.C., for example, the last Greek king of Kabul became a Chinese vassal. When they were unable to conquer the most powerful of their enemies, they signed treaties of alliance as well as trade agreements with them. It was thus they gained the services of the bellicose Kushans who dominated the Gandhara and the Transoxiana regions, the unavoidable passage for all westward bound caravans in the first and second centuries. Thanks to this agreement the route to the west was wide open to the Chinese merchants.

Silk made its appearance in the Western world towards the beginning of the Christian era, thanks to the Romans who had discovered it in the Middle East. This material, however, was not unknown to the Mediterraneans. Indeed, in the fourth century B.C. Alexander the Great's soldiers, after conquering Persia and reaching the western boundary of India, had brought back with them "magic threads" with which magnificent clothes could be made. But they had been forgotten. Four centuries later, the Silk Route, or rather, the various Silk, Spice and Rice Routes, experienced a period of unprecedented economic growth. Thousands of caravans began to pass each other on this complex network of roads between the Far East and Europe.

*General view and detail of a **medressa**, Registan Place in Samarcande, Uzbekistan, formerly one of the most important stop-overs on the northern branch of the Silk Route.*

A WELL-KEPT SECRET

Meanwhile, silk had taken on considerable importance in the Middle Empire. Not only was it used to make different materials (gauze, crepon, brocade, velvet and shantung), paper and ropes, but the Chinese sovereigns had also become accustomed to paying their troops with bolts of silk. Since a large part of their armies were composed of mercenaries who, once they were paid, returned home to Manchuria, Persia, Siberia or India and displayed these rare, and thus expensive, iridescent materials, a craze for these fabrics developed among their compatriots. Still, the secret of how silk was made was jealously kept by the imperial craftsmen, thus making it even more precious. The traitor or the imprudent person who revealed all or part of the manufacturing techniques of this all but divine material was immediately put to death. Silk was so valuable that it soon became the absolute currency standard for imperial trade. As contacts with India, Persia and Arabia multiplied, it naturally became the Chinese product in greatest demand. In the eyes of the world, China was the country of silk.

Silk Enters the Western World

$\mathcal{T}$he Romans, as we have seen,
were the first Westerners to rediscover silk. This took place in the Middle East in dramatic circumstances.
In 53 B.C. their legions were about to confront the powerful Parthian army at Carrhae on the Euphrates.
Suddenly the Parthians unfurled immense brightly colored silk banners.
The Roman legions were overcome by panic and fled.

ROMAN REALISM

$\mathcal{H}$alf a century later, after numerous reversals and difficulties , Rome succeeded in pushing the Parthians far off to the east. Rome then sent its administration and colonists to settle in the Middle East. These new-comers witnessed the favor silk enjoyed in the Eastern courts. As shrewd tradesmen, they quickly realized the advantage it could procure them. Their merchants undertook to bring back to Rome the prestigious silk material that had so frightened their soldiers in the past. In Italy it met with immediate success, first with the fashionably dressed women of the capital and then throughout the Empire. No doubt, through a distortion of the Chinese word, "seu", silk was called "serica", and China, the land of the Seres, the silk manufacturers.

By the middle of the first century, Imperial Rome, already the greatest military and trading power of the Mediterranean, launched into the profitable silk trade. Its armies had just annexed Pontus, Syria and Palestine. They had crossed the Tigris and Euphrates Rivers and

had defeated the Persians. A flow of jewelry, works of art, fabrics and carpets went from the subjected regions toward the Italian cities ever eager for more. The Roman merchants were principally supplied by Persian and Arab sailors, but they sought to establish more direct relations by land with those unknown countries where silk was manufactured. Between them lay the obstacle of the powerful states of central Asia, among which, the inevitable Parthians, who controlled the caravan routes. The Romans prevailed over them definitively in the third century. Through the intermediary of the Parthian empire, henceforth the forced allies of Rome, they finally gained access to the routes to the east.
The importance of the central Asian peoples in the development of the land routes must not be underestimated. Directly or indirectly they became Rome's preferred trading partners in this part of the world, despite the many local wars they fought with each other. At the beginning of the Christian era, the Silk Route experienced an unprecedented economic boom, thanks to the stability of the four empires - Rome, China, and between them the Parthians and the Kushans.

A Pakistani from Thatta.
An Afghan from Danlatabad.

THE MARITIME ROUTE

After the end of the first century, trade along the Silk Route was flourishing. Yet, at either end of this fantastic economic chain the people hardly knew each other. Thus, the Romans established a clear difference between the Thinai, the "real" Chinese that their traders and soldiers had come across in the Middle East, and the mysterious Seres. There were the most extravagant rumors going round about the Seres. It was said that silk grew on trees inhabited by gods, and that the Seres might live to be centuries old. As reputable an author as Pliny described them as "giants… with blue eyes and red hair!" As for the Chinese, they were highly impressed by what they heard about the social organization and the military power of the Romans. They called them the Great Qins, which was their way of recognizing the Romans as equals.
From the second century on, the maritime trade increased, due to the insecurity prevailing in central Asia, which had been devastated by frequent wars and whose roads were constantly threatened by bands of brigands; and due also to the growing pretensions of the Kushans, who demanded increasingly substantial tribute to let the caravans cross their lands. Although maritime routes had existed for as long as the roads, the general political conditions had reduced them to a minor role. If truth be told, traveling by sea was not in the least a sinecure. The trail that went from Antioch to Xi' by land was 15,000 kilometers long and it took about nine months to cover it. The distance by sea was twice as long and the dangers one encountered, from storms to pirates, were even more formidable. Merchants only took it under duress, when they had no alternative because the situation in central Asia was so bad that caravans could not get through. Leaving Rome, the goods were loaded, bound for Alexandria. It then took another two or three weeks before they could be carried by caravan to Red Sea ports. There, they were again loaded on boats going to the Indian coast, where Indian or Malaysian merchants purchased them. They then had the choice of dispatching them to China along the overland route or hugging the Indian, Burmese, Indochinese and finally the Chinese coasts.
Despite the multiple difficulties, at the end of the third century there was, nevertheless, as much maritime traffic as there was land traffic.

THE SECRET REVEALED

By the end of the fourth century total control of the trade routes linking the Far East and central Asia was in the hands of the Chinese, although this had been delayed by certain sinister episodes of third century Chinese history, such as the division of the Middle Empire into three rival states, called the Three Realms, and numerous barbarian invasions from the north, including the bellicose Xiongnu. All of these small dynasties were in a permanent state of war. The strongest, the Wei Pei dynasty, finally managed to lay down the law and to establish unity through a fairly stable empire in the north. At the same time, south of the Huanghe four dynasties of Chinese origin, among whom were the Sungs, began the fantastic economic boom that was a prelude to the future Sung Empire. The safety and development of the trade routes went hand in hand with the consolidation of power in the two zones separated by the great river. By now practically deified, silk was yielding enormous returns to the imperial thrones. The Roman and Kushan Empires had fallen, and the White Huns had devastated central Asia where the general situation remained quite chaotic. Slowly but surely the Weis of the north were extending their power towards the west by skillfully alternating armed expeditions with alliances. The Sungs of the south continued to develop one of the most brilliant cultures China had ever known.

In the fifth century, however, an event took place which deprived silk of all its wonder. According to tradition, a young Chinese princess, who had been promised in marriage to the King of Khotan, an oasis principality along the Silk Route, was disconsolate at the thought of having to leave China for a country where silk weaving was unknown. Unbearable! So, hidden in her chignon, she took along silkworm eggs and mulberry leaves, thus introducing sericulture to Khotan. And from there, around the year 550 A.D., Nestorian monks stole the precious caterpillars and seeds, concealing them in their hollow canes, and brought them to Constantinople. And that is how the thousand-year-old secret of Chinese silk was revealed to the world. Thereafter, silk no longer had its divine character. It was simply a valuable material.

MUTUAL EXCHANGES IN THE LATE MIDDLE AGES

Trade between Europe and the Far East was at its zenith between the seventh and tenth centuries during the dynasty of the Tangs whose reign covered the golden age of Chinese culture. The Tangs extended their domination over eastern central Asia, northern Vietnam, Mongolia and southern Manchuria. Their capital, Xi'an, known at the time as Chang'an was, with its 500,00 inhabitants, the cultural center of Asia. Meanwhile, in Europe a veritable silk industry had been set up, not only in Italy which had the trade monopoly thanks to Venice, Genoa and Pisa, but also in Greece, Spain and even in France where silk workshops were mushrooming. The exchanges between Europe and the Far East were attaining a heretofore unequaled level.

It is obvious that if the maritime and overland routes were so successful, it is because the trade was profitable for everyone. Silk, porcelain, laquors, ceramics, spices, gems, precious wood, furs and medicinal plants, many of which, like rhubarb, had previously been unknown, all arrived on the Mediterranean markets from China, India and Siberia. Mediterranean coral the Chinese women were so fond of, ivory, ostrich feathers and eggs from Africa, myrrh and incense from Arabia, carpets and henna from Persia, lapis lazuli from Afghanistan and horses from central Asia all were dispatched in the opposite direction, to the Middle Empire.

ARTISTS AND PILGRIMS

Merchandise was not the only commodity to take advantage of the exceptional Silk Route network. Art and religion, food for the mind, soon began the same journey. In this way the Middle Empire was influenced by several of the great religions. Coming from India, Buddhism and its magnificent artistic forms of expression, penetrated into the heartland of China and reached Mongolia where it was enthusiastically adopted by the people. Then, other religious

A Kirghiz nomad.
An old Uighur medicine man from Kashgar.

persuasions, mainly from Persia, such as Mazdaism and Manicheanism, were introduced into the western part of the country. Finally, Christian Nestorianism, after conquering parts of Persia and India, spread to China.

The last religion to set foot in China in the eighth century was Islam. It was also the one that best resisted imperial power. Following the Muslim conquests in central Asia, Islam took solid root in western China. But it also reached into southern China in the territory of the rich Sungs via seaports, particularly Canton, where Arab merchants frequently dropped anchor. In fact, all of the maritime trade between the Persian Gulf, the Indian Ocean and the China Sea was controlled by the Arabs. The powerful courts in Cairo, Damascus, Baghdad and Basra needed, and therefore greatly contributed to, the development of this trade. Conversely, many Chinese merchant junks could be seen in the ports of the Arabic peninsula and the Middle East. The former Rice Route acquired great economic importance.

In the tenth century a series of imperial decrees banned all foreign religions from Chinese lands, causing the Chinese to withdraw suddenly into their shells. Only Islam and Nestorianism succeeded in maintaining their influence on the western and northern edges of the Empire and in central Asia. These lands, where Nestorianism had taken root, gave birth to the legend of the Kingdom of Prester John, a Christian priest-king who defeated the Muslims. This myth, also mentioned in *Description of the World*, circulated throughout Western Europe during the Middle Ages.

A Tibetan Champa.

The fragile compromise between the Khitan and the Sungs

The best guarantee for east - west commerce was the stability of the Middle Empire. Any military or political disturbance in China brought immediate repercussions to international exchanges. From the tenth to the twelfth centuries the Pei Sung, or the northern Sungs, dominated all of China except for the northernmost areas, beyond present day Beijing, which remained in the hands of the Khitan. During this unprecedented era, the country saw the appearance of wood engraving and the development of porcelain and silk painting. The Pei Sung capital of K'ai'fong (present-day Kaifeng) was home to over seven hundred thousand people, which made it the most highly populated city in the world. But the Sung Empire was soon to be threatened on its northern and western borders by barbarian peoples. To the north the Khitan founded the Liao dynasty, while to the east the Tangut, a Turco-Mongolian people created the kingdom of Xi Xia. During the course of the eleventh century the Sung emperors purchased peace from their bellicose neighbors in exchange for heavy yearly tributes. Peace having been thus ensured, exceptional patronage kept art and literature, as well as the sciences, thriving. Chinese scholarship and technology were far superior to those of Europe.

At the beginning of the twelfth century, however, new barbarians, the Juchen (or Jürchen), arrived from the north. Tired of paying tributes to the Khitan, the Sungs seized the opportunity. They entered into an alliance with the Juchen and had them attack the Khitan. The latter were indeed beaten, but the Juchen took up the Khitan's demands for themselves. They created the Chin dynasty and undertook to march on Kaifeng. Their armies met hardly any opposition. They captured the capital and took the Sung emperor prisoner. Gao Zong, one of the monarch's sons, managed to flee across the Huanghe where he founded the new empire of the southern Sungs. He chose Hang'tcheou (present-day Hangzhou) for his capital and continued to resist the Juchen. The city became an important river port thanks to its location on the coast at one end of the Grand Canal that linked it to northern China. This period saw the renaissance of Chinese philosophy and painting. Trade did not suffer from the difficult relations between the north and the south and continued to prosper.

The Polo Family

Dominating the Jiayu pass is the Jiayuguan fort with its high wooden towers. At the end of the Ming period it was the westernmost portion of the Great Wall.

While traffic on the maritime route continued to increase, that of the overland caravan roads hardly changed. The long journey, the climatic hardships in the various lands they crossed, the political instability of central Asia and the permanent threat of looters were some of the obstacles to the development of the overland routes.

THE CRUSADES : CATALYSTS OF THE OVERLAND ROUTES

But, in the year 1096, Pope Urbin II assigned to the European Crusaders the mission of freeing the holy places in Palestine. The expedition saw the fall of Jerusalem and was the first of eight Crusades which were to build up the overseas kingdom. Tens of thousands of soldiers set out on the roads to the Middle East, with merchants following close behind. Among the latter, the Italians (Venetians and especially Genovese) were the most pugnacious. At first, they were content to transport the necessary provisions and materiel to the Crusaders already in the field; then they founded counting houses and warehouses throughout the eastern Mediterranean. Finally, they established close contacts with eastern merchants and devised with them a well-structured system of exchanges. Land trade was suddenly back in favor. At last, to meet wartime needs, the western network of roads rivaled that of the east. At the end of the twelfth century, most trade followed the central and northern Silk

Routes as well as the Spice Route in the south. In Europe, the implacable rivalry for exclusive control of the western sector of this lucrative trade continued to grow among Venice, Genoa and Pisa. The economic struggle eventually degenerated into an undeclared war. At times the secret maneuvers brought about tragic consequences. The Venetians, for example, for both political and financial reasons, directed the fourth Crusade towards Zara and then Constantinople, capital of the Byzantine Empire whose economic power hampered them. After unscrupulously seizing everything they came upon, the Venetians then established their economic domination of the region, thus securing control of both the northern and the central Routes for themselves. Among those pioneer traders was one Marco Polo, later known as Marco the Elder, to distinguish him from his illustrious nephew.

THE MONGOL STAKES

In China, the Sungs and the Chins seemed satisfied with the existing status quo when a new assailant arrived from the north at the head of hordes of Tartar horsemen. This invader was much more dangerous than all of those who had preceded him. His name was Temudjin. His striking victories over the Kereyits, the Merkits, the Naimans and the Tanguts had earned him the title of Genghis Khan, supreme head of the Tartars. Nothing was able to stop the inexorable march of his troops who crushed in rapid succession the Liaos, the Ouzbeks, the Afghans, the Turks of Khorassan, the Russians and the Persians. Genghis Khan meet his fate in 1227. His empire was divided into large family fiefs. The three most powerful were, in the west, the Khans of Persia, in southern Russia, the Golden Horde and in the east, the Yuans, who settled in northern China. They all continued Genghis Khan's work, sending their armies to wage war in eastern Europe, in the Middle East and the Mediterranean. In China, the Yuans, led by the Great Khans Mongka and then Kubilai, destroyed the Chin Empire and then captured Kaifeng, before sweeping on to the south. Europe was in a state of terror at the threat of the invincible Tartars, who had just invaded the plains of Hungary and had crossed the Carpathian Mountains and about whom the most terrifying stories circulated. Moreover, the situation in the Holy Land was catastrophic. The Crusaders were being beaten by the Saracens and were losing their fortresses one after the other. Islam threatened to conquer the Mediterranean. Then suddenly, incredible news reached them from the East. The terrible Mongols were attacking the Muslims ! In 1221 their armies had annihilated the great kingdoms of Khorassan. In 1258, Hulagu, Genghis Khan's grandson, captured Baghdad and eliminated the caliphate. Europe and the Vatican suddenly saw yesterday's enemies turned into potential allies as they defeated the Mohammedans. Public opinion even went so far as to present the Mongol sovereigns as the descendants of King David. For both kings and popes, entering into an alliance with this military power became a priority. The former encouraged their merchants to develop trade with the Mongol authorities, whereas the latter sent religious emissaries to try to convert the Tartar leaders. The adventures of Marco Polo took place in this context. Indeed, the Polos set off for Mongol territory in the name of Christendom.

A Mongol horse breeder.

A young Dravidian from Kerala.

THE FIRST EUROPEAN VISITORS TO CHINA

The Polos were not the first Europeans to visit China. Some merchants and missionaries had penetrated the western reaches of the Middle Empire before them. The Yuan government allowed caravan trade, which had long been confiscated by the victorious Arabs and the Uighurs, to resume in central Asia. Chinese bankers and merchants vigorously backed the action of the Mongols, who, after Genghis Khan, had shown a great interest in trade. Concessions were abolished; peace on the roads was guaranteed by the omnipresence of the army, and an ingenious communications system based on that of the Mongol post was established. At that time, two main routes led to China: the northern route went through the Crimea, following the River Don and then the Volga, passing through Kazakhstan and Dzoungary before reaching Kashgar where it took the Gobi Desert trail to Khan-balik (present-day Peking or Beijing). The southern route went through the Middle East, Persia, Transoxiana, the Tarim Basin and, following the course of the Yellow River, headed north to Khan-balik. It was not safe until 1260 when Hulagu conquered Persia and the Middle East. It was all the more safe as the northern route had come under the control of the Mongol sovereigns of the Golden Horde which had recently converted to Islam and were no longer in agreement with the central power.

During the first half of the thirteenth century, European travelers generally followed the northern route, controlled by the Mongols, thus avoiding the southern territories held by the Muslims. This is the way Jean Plan du Carpin of Lyons went in 1245, bringing the Great Khan Kuyuk a letter from the Pope; he was followed by André Longjumeau in 1249 and Guillaume de Rubroek in 1254. These three were the saintly King Louis's special envoys to the Mongol emperors. But all they obtained, particularly from the new Great Khan Mongka, was a letter asking the king of France to pledge allegiance to the Mongol sovereign.

When the northern route became more dangerous, European travelers and missionaries became accustomed to taking the one to the south. Among these illustrious travelers, one name in particular was to engage unanimous attention, that of the Polos, a Venetian family of merchants whose destiny was to surprise the world.

A young beauty from Sigiriya, Sri Lanka.

A young girl from the Lisu tribe in Yunnan.

THE POLOS OF VENICE

The proud city of Venice was home to the best bankers and merchants Italy produced at that time. The extremely wealthy Ziani family lived there, competing with the powerful Dandolos, Gradenigos and Zenos. The Polo family was of only modest importance. According to contemporary documents, the first Polos are believed to have left the Italian warehouses on the Dalmatian coast in 1033 to settle in Venice. A century later several other Polos appeared in the city of the Doges although it is impossible to establish a certain kinship among them. Nevertheless, we know today that the Polo brothers, Marco, that is Marco the Elder, Niccolo and Maffeo (Venetian for the Italian Matteo), as well as their sister Flora, were descendants of a branch of the family from the San Trovaso quarter. Marco the Elder was the first to leave his native town to set up a warehouse in Constantinople. He even opened a branch in Soldaia (present-day Sudak) in the Crimea, to trade in furs. Niccolo and Maffeo, on the contrary, had chosen to trade in precious stones. They set off in 1254 to join their elder brother in Constantinople in order to develop the family business. Niccolo left behind him his pregnant wife, whose name remains unknown. A few months after Niccolo's departure, the baby was born. He was named Marco, after his senior uncle.

NICCOLO AND MAFFEO POLO'S FIRST VOYAGE

Laden with riches, the two brothers' ships rounded southern Greece, traveled northwards to the Hellespont (the Dardanelles) before coming into port in Constantinople. They had intended to stay in the prestigious city for several months only, but they remained for six years. They traded essentially in precious stones. However, the veiled political rivalries of Constantinople, fed by the eternal competition between Venetians and Genovese were threatening to degenerate into open warfare. The fate of the Byzantine capital was soon going to be sealed. The new Greek emperor was waiting for an opportunity to seize the ancient city. Disinclined to stay in such a troubled atmosphere the two brothers decided to set out to the east, to Soldaia, where they would join Marco the Elder. Meanwhile, in Venice Niccolo's wife had died and young Marco was taken in by his aunt Flora and her husband Zane. The couple and their three sons and one daughter settled into Marco's home, the latter constantly awaiting his father's return, though he had had no news of him.

Niccolo and Maffeo, on the other hand, quickly realized that there was little money to be earned in Soldaia. They decided to leave the shores of the Black Sea and to pursue their way as far as the Volga. This river defined the westernmost border of the kingdom of Berka Khan, Genghis Khan's grandson and the first Mongol ruler to convert to Islam. He was the master of the Golden Horde which got its name from its wealth and its members' immoderate craving for the precious metal. Trading, whenever the opportunity arose, in precious stones, salt, fur and perhaps even slaves, the Polo brothers made their way northeastward. They reached Bolgara (present-day Bulgar), the summer residence of the western Tartars, where they were sumptuously welcomed by Berke. In exchange for the jewels the two brothers presented him, he gave them gifts worth twice as much. Niccolo and Maffeo, under the Khan's protection, were able to take advantage of the situation to do some profitable business in the Golden Horde territories for a whole year.

A M'nong from Vietnam.

Just when they wished to return to Constantinople, war broke out between Berke and his cousin Hulagu, leader of the Tartar Empire of the Levant in Persia. An important battle took place in 1262 and 1263, without either side carrying off the victory. But the way back to Europe had been cut off and the Polos took to the road again, heading eastward; they soon arrived at Bucara (present-day Bukhara), an important trading center along the Silk Route. The war between the Tartars, however, was soon to catch up with them there. For three years they were stranded in the city, doing business when they could. It was here in Bucara that they met an emissary of Hulagu returning from a mission in Persia. The Mongol nobleman was surprised and fascinated by these Latins, about whom he had heard, but who had hardly ever been seen in central Asia, and he brought them to Karakorum, the summer capital of "the lord of all the Tartars," Kubilai Khan. After a year-long journey across Asia, the travelers arrived at the court of the Great Khan. They were the first secular Europeans to visit the Middle Empire. The Mongol sovereign was very interested in the political and religious customs of the West. He asked thousands of questions of the two brothers who endeavored to satisfy his curiosity. When they were ready to leave, Kubilai Khan handed them a message for the Pope asking him to send to China "up to one hundred wise men capable of teaching Christian religion and doctrine" to his Tartars. Protected by the golden tablets which served as a safe conduct, Niccolo and Maffeo made the return trip through the western territories, arriving in Ayas (present-day Payas) on the Gulf of Alexandrette three years later. From there they embarked for Acre which they reached in 1269. Meanwhile, Pope Clement IV had died. They told the tale of their journey to Tedaldo Visconti the papal legate in Palestine, but he was unwilling to undertake anything without consulting the new pontiff. They thus had to wait for the papal election before answering Kubilai. As the decision was long in coming, the two brothers chose to return to Venice. There Niccolo learned of his wife's death and discovered Marco, the fifteen-year-old son he had never seen.

For two years the Polo brothers remained in Venice awaiting the election of Clement IV's successor. Niccolo remarried; his wife was Fiordelise Trevisan. Marco finally was living with the father he had so missed as a child. The new Pope still had not been elected. Fearing that Kubilai Khan would grow angry with the delay, the two men decided to return to Tartary. In 1271 they set off once again for the East, but this time they brought along with them a new companion eager for adventure, young Marco.

The seventeen-year-old Venetian could not have suspected that he was setting off on the most fantastic journey known to mankind.

Aerial view of a dromedary market in India.
One can imagine what the great fairs must have been like in Marco Polo's times.

1271 - 1275
the Journey to the East

In Acre, two weeks after leaving Venice,
the Polos once again met the legate Tedaldo Visconti who provided them with papal letters and credentials.
They traveled on to Jerusalem "to get a little oil from the lamp in the Holy Sepulcher,
as the Great Khan had requested," then finally set off for Ayas.
As soon as they arrived in the city, they learned that a new pontiff had finally been appointed; it was their old
acquaintance Tedaldo Visconti, who came to the Christian throne as Gregory X. They were instantly called back to Acre
by a papal messenger. His Holiness the Pope intended to entrust them with an official mission to Tartar territory in the
name of Christendom. They were not only to win the confidence of the Great Khan and to encourage him to ally himself
with the Christians against the Muslims, but they were also to attempt to convert him to Christianity.
To accompany them and help them in their task, the Pope gave them
"two Dominican friars who were indeed the wisest and the most worthy of the province."
He also presented them with "licenses, charters and letters with full powers, [...] numerous crystal jewels and other gifts
to give to the Great Khan." The little group set out on its way to Ayas, aware of the importance of its mission.
Gregory X had entrusted them with the hopes of the whole of Europe.
They had to succeed at all costs. To do so they would travel almost 10,000 kilometers,
crossing unknown and hostile regions for six long years.

Two Armenias and Turcomanie

FROM CENTRAL TURKEY TO ARMENIA

A typical village in the Ceyhan region where there is still an active community of Armenian origin.

The houses were built atop the hill as a defensive measure.

*The Polos had finished preparing for their journey.
In Ayas, a trading center located on the Gulf of Alexandrette, young Marco found himself on familiar ground.
Indeed, what is today a sleepy market town was then the starting point for eastbound travelers.
It was overflowing with Genovese and Venetian merchants.
Its port was the main outlet for goods transported by caravans arriving from Persia, central Asia and Cathay,
as Europeans then called northern China.*

THE ADANA REGION

Along with Adana and Tarsus, Ayas was one of the principal cities of Lesser Armenia, formerly called Cilicia. This region, today part of Turkey, corresponded to the Adana plain and to its mountainous back-country. Armenians fleeing Greater Armenia after it was overrun by the Byzantines in the eleventh century had settled here and given the country its name. They had founded a small independent state allied to the Crusaders which lasted until the end of the fourteenth century. Just as the Polos were about to embark, alarming news arrived from Ayas. Baybars, the sultan of the Mamelukes, was threatening Armenia. The two Dominicans, Marco tells us "in dread of advancing any further, fearing for their lives [...] gave all the licenses, letters and presents the Pope had entrusted them with to Messer Niccolo and Messer Maffeo [...] and took off for Acre by sea."

Abandoned by their companions, the Polos thereafter found themselves alone to face their destiny. This was in the spring of 1272. Slowly, the caravan got under way, heading northwest through Lesser Armenia. Marco recorded that "there are many cities, castles and villages and all things are plentiful" in this area, but regretted that the people were "puny and lowly [...] great gluttons and drinkers." The unflattering opinion the Venetian had of the inhabitants was due to the bad reputation of the local aristocracy who were accused of

The mountains of Lebanon face the Mediterranean Sea.

Deep into Syria there are innumerable fortified castles; here, the Krak des Chevaliers, constructed during the Crusades.

delighting in inordinate luxury and giving themselves up to all sorts of political intrigues. The general population, by contrast, was hard-working and attached to their traditions and suffered from the practices of the upper classes and the consequences thereof.

What remains today of the places and cultures that Marco visited? Lesser Armenia is still composed of an immense alluvial plain, watered by two great rivers, the Seyhan and the Ceyhan and bordered on its right by the Amanos Mountains. Stifling in the summer, this fertile plain is covered with fields of cotton, wheat, citrus fruits, market gardens and rice

One of the famous giant mushrooms in Cappadocia, a vast plateau of volcanic tufa that have been eroded by winds and rivers for hundreds of thousands of years.

paddies, which make it one of the richest farming regions in Turkey. Historical remains of the past are rare; they were destroyed by the recurring wars between the Byzantines and the Arabs. Although there is still a very strong Armenian community jealously protecting its ancient rites in the region of Adana, the majority of the population is a mixture of Kurds and former Turkmen nomads that settled here during the nineteenth century.

CENTRAL TURKEY

After leaving Lesser Armenia the Polo caravan entered the province of Turkestan. Marco Polo's Turkestan corresponds exactly to today's central Turkey. The region is famous for the exceptional beauty of its landscapes, particularly in the western part, better known as Cappadocia. This plateau, with its rugged volcanic massifs and deep fertile valleys is inhabited by highly mixed populations; the original peoples were undoubtedly of Indo-European stock, who later mingled with successive waves of Hittites, Phrygians and Persians, and after that with Turkmens and Kurds.

*Despite its apparent aridity and moon-like quality,
the center of Turkey has a large network of rivers
that makes raising livestock possible;
the valleys produce rich harvests of cereals, fruits and grapes.*

*These tiny, often very poor, hamlets
are built around their mosques and can be found scattered
among the strange jagged forms of Cappadocia.*

In Marco Polo's time, the inhabitants of these wild lands were essentially nomads known as Turcomans or Turkmens who, *Description of the World* tells us "worship Mohamet and obey his law [...]. They roam over the mountains and plains, where they can find good pastures for their sheep, for they do not work the land, but live solely from livestock."

The country is still inhabited by these peoples of Turkmen origin who in all probability came from western Kazakhstan. They have been joined, through the vicissitudes of history, by many other ethnic groups. One thus finds Armenians and Greeks of Indo-European and Mediterranean origin, and numerous Turkic ethnic groups belonging to the Altaic family.

Before the seventh century, central Turkey had a dense Christian population. It was the crossroads of north-south and east-west trade.
During this period of economic growth, it was exposed to cross-currents of the major religions.

*From that exceptional era
Turkey has preserved a great
many churches and monasteries
decorated with superb Byzantine
and Nestorian wall paintings.*

EASTERN TURKEY

Greater Armenia, as described by Marco Polo, consisted of a vast region spreading from Central Turkey to the borders of present-day Armenia. It was adjacent to contemporary Georgia, which is the southern part of today's Azerbaijan. This picturesque region presents a jagged relief. The ample folds of the Taurus Mountains to the south and the Pontic Mountains to the north join together in one powerful mountain chain over 2,000 meters in altitude. The Greater Armenia visited by the Polos no longer exists. Formerly an important kingdom, it partially collapsed in the eleventh century under the pressure of the Byzantine armies. The final blow was delivered in 1375 by the Turks and the Mongols. Best known for Mount Ararat where, according to the legend, Noah's ark ran aground, Greater Armenia was also a rich province of the Tartar empire. Here Marco Polo admired the "best buckrams in the world," that is, the valuable cotton and brocade fabrics. The inhabitants earned their living from the income produced by their cotton and livestock. Little has changed in this part of the world where modernity has been making slow progress. In the tiny villages of eastern Turkey one still

The head of Apollo-Mithras
overlooks the arid valleys of western Turkey, home of the Kurds.

finds the country's most beautiful traditional fabrics. Likewise, the economy still relies heavily on sheep raising and its by-products. Approaching the thirteenth century Georgian border, Marco Polo heard reports of a nearby "spring from which wells up an oily liquid [...] (which) is not good to eat, but which is good for burning and rubbing on men and animals affected with itching." Of course, they were referring to petroleum. Our traveler was the first Westerner to indicate its existence to his contemporaries. The substratum of eastern Turkey, Azerbaijan and northern Iraq contain immense petroleum deposits which, since extraction began after the Second World War, have contributed considerably to the development of these economies. When the Polo caravan crossed Greater Armenia, it was inhabited by Armenians, friends of

The Nemrut Dag is the colossal sanctuary built by Antiochos of Kommagenes
during the first century B.C. in the foothills of the Anti-Taurus mountains at an altitude of 2,500 meters.
Searches by local inhabitants and teams of scientists have still not revealed the ruler's tomb.

Bas-relief in Arsameia showing Heracles welcoming King Mithridates.

the Venetians for over two hundred years. Their kings had signed a treaty of alliance with the Republic of Venice that simply confirmed the excellent cultural and trade relations the rulers of Armenia had maintained with the Venetians since the end of the tenth century.

Many monophysitic Christians and Muslims lived side by side with the Armenians with whom they were on good terms. The former believed that the divine and the human were united in one sole entity, Christ. Judged heretical by the Roman Church at the Council of Chalcedon in 451, their doctrine, together with certain traces of the ancient rites, can, nevertheless, still be discerned in some eastern Christian churches, hidden within the general syncretism.

Going southeastward, one crosses the mountain ranges that continue into neighboring Azerbaijan.
Even further south, the compact mass of the Zagros Mountains is covered by a thick layer of snow in winter.
This range, which runs to the Persian Gulf, contains a number of peaks that are over 4,000 meters high. ▷

Leaving Turkey, one comes to this Iranian wilderness.
Although quite arid in summer, it is, nevertheless,
of exceptional beauty. This region is beset with serious political
and military conflicts and is slowly losing its population.

The Eight Kingdoms of Persia

FROM WESTERN IRAN TO AFGHANISTAN

"You must know that in Persia
there are eight kingdoms [...]. When merchants from these lands travel from one country to another,
they traverse vast deserts, that is to say, dry, barren, sandy regions where no grass or fodder suitable for horses grows [...].
So they use asses, for they are lively and swift steeds [...] and also camels,
which likewise carry heavy loads and are cheap to maintain."

THE TARTAR EMPIRE OF PERSIA

This is how *Description of the World* presents Marco Polo's thirteenth century Persia. The eight royal cities, Kasvin, Kurdistan, Luristan, Shulistan, Isfahan, Shiraz, Shabankara and Tun and Kain correspond approximately to the present-day cities and regions of Qazvin, Kurdistan, Luristan, Ispahan, Fars and Khorassan. They were more like provinces and geographical regions than actual kingdoms; most of the administrative boundaries have been adopted by Iran today.

Persia, as Marco Polo found it, already had little in common with the great Persian empire whose grandeur had dominated the world from the sixth century B.C. to the seventh century A.D. After first tenaciously resisting the Romans, and then the Byzantines, the Sassanians finally succumbed to the attacks of the Muslim Arabs.

Persia became part of the Omayyad empire, then came under the domination of the Abbasids in the eighth century. Two centuries later the Turks, who were already masters of Khorassan, conquered the entire country, making it the cultural leader of the Seljukian world. But in 1220 - 1221 Genghis Khan and the Mongols swept through the region.

By the time the Polos had arrived in Persia, all of the provinces were part of the Tartar empire. Hulagu and his successor's troops had just ravaged the countryside, destroyed the towns and massacred whole Muslim populations. The Christian community had been spared by the personal order of Hulagu's wife. The Polos were thus crossing a country in the throes of reconstruction.

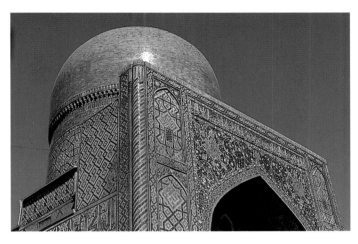

The great Muslim period of Persian art
began at the end of the seventh century. Its great architectural
and pictorial achievements were miniatures, as well as the domes
and cupolas of mosques and palaces. From Iran to central Asia
there is an infinite diversity of forms, mosaics and colors
in the art work created under the influence of the Persians.

The long steppe-covered plains west of Kuh-e Rud are home to sheep and goat herders.

INHOSPITABLE DESERTS AND POOR POPULATIONS

Like our Venetian travelers, the modern visitor is struck by the great expanse of desert regions and the hard living conditions. The contrast between the peasants' poverty and the city-dwellers' opulence is even more pronounced at the end of the twentieth century than in Marco Polo's time. He described in great detail the beastly heat and the sandstorms. The road he took is the one that descends from Tabriz in the northwest towards Kerman in the southeast. To the right it follows the impressive Zagros Mountains that dominate rocky red outcroppings. To the left is the endless expanse of the arid, colorless Iranian desert, the Dasht-e Lut.

The peoples living there in the thirteenth century are the same as today. They can be divided into three groups : the poor semi-nomads surviving on the income from their lean sheep and goat herds, the slightly richer farmers, who support themselves through subsistence farming and livestock raising, and finally the city-dwellers, some of whom are quite wealthy and whose interests and education are Western. The economic gap is enormous, particularly between the urban population which, although only a minority, controls the country's economy, and the majority of Iranians who eke out a meager existence. These masses of peasants and workers provide the natural breeding ground for the governing theocracy. Political and religious manipulation of the uneducated masses has always been the basis of the ayatollahs' policy.

The mountain foothills and the secondary bottomlands contain many hamlets with poor populations; here, near Yazd.

During the winter the high plateaus become vast white deserts
and for nearly three months life moves at a slow pace.

In the center of Iran is a series of long sedimentary alluvial plains. Where irrigation systems have been built, farming and livestock raising are the main activities. Elsewhere, the desert reigns master.

The influence of the **mullahs**,
doctors of the Koranic faith,
has increased considerably among Shiites,
especially since the founding
of the Islamic Republic in 1979.

During the Achura holiday
which takes place on the tenth day of the new year,
Shiites commemorate the martyrdom of emir Husayn.
They inflict terrible penance on themselves,
lacerating their backs and shoulders
with razor sharp blades.

In public, Iranian women must wear the Muslim veil,
the large traditional black veil
that covers them to their ankles.

FORMIDABLE SHIITES

Like contemporary Iranians, the Persians Marco Polo met were mostly Shiites. Our Venetian judged them as people who were xenophobic, even aggressively so, very traditional and observant of a strict form of Islam. Even today, traveling in Iran is not an easy undertaking, especially for women. The many obligations and prohibitions imposed upon foreigners in the name of religion substantially reduce the pleasure one has in visiting this superb country.

The landscape is sumptuous and the cities abound in innumerable ancient, often totally neglected, monuments .

Ever since Iran became the Islamic Republic of Iran, religion and mores are no longer to be taken lightly. Apparently this was not the case when Marco Polo was there.

According to him, one could come to terms with Koranic law. People ate grapes and drank wine since, "they understood the text of their law (Islam) to mean that if the wine is boiled so that it is partly consumed, they are free to drink it without breaching the law or the commandments."

FIRE WORSHIPERS

In a small village in Persia called Ataperistan, Marco Polo came across strange believers who "worshiped fire". They were, in fact, adepts of Zoroastrianism, the world's oldest religion still practiced. It was founded by the prophet Zarathustra or Zoroaster who reformed the ancient Mazda faith seven centuries before the Christian era. The faithful, known as "Ghebr" in Iran and "Parsi" in Pakistan and India, worshiped light as a symbol of absolute goodness. They honored its most obvious manifestation, fire. For over 2,500 years a flame has been kept alive in Zoroastrian shrines; it has even been authorized in Shiite Iran. In India their community plays an important economic role. Certain Parsi families, like the Tata of Bombay, are among the richest in the world.

As a good Christian, Marco, although enchanted by the religion's pacifism and tolerance, felt obliged to draw it into the Christian circle one way or another. He claimed to have found an explanation for this unusual faith. According to legend, the three Wise Men came bearing gifts for the Christ child. Once they had given the gold, myrrh and incense to the divine infant and were about to return to their respective countries they were presented with "a closed casket and told not to open it." The three Wise Men's curiosity, however, soon overtook them. They opened the casket only to discover a stone inside. Convinced that they

The priest's face is covered by a piece of material so that his breath does not soil the purity of the sacred fire. The woman's sari is attached in the old style, by a brooch on her left shoulder. This type of clothing is no longer worn in public in Iran.

Two of the most sacred symbols of Zoroastrianism : winged guardians of the celestial realm and fravashi, *representing the spiritual protector that looks after each human being.*

were being mocked, they threw the stone down a well where it immediately burst into flame.
The inhabitants kept this miraculous fire and decided never to let it die.
To add further authenticity to his story, Marco added that he had been to Sava (present-day Saveh) and had personally visited the tombs of Balthazar, Gaspard and Melchior.

In a lush green oasis on the sides of Kuh-e Hazaran,
the deserted citadel Arg e Bam overlooks the old city of the same name.
Founded at the time of the Sassanians and reconstructed in the twelfth century, this imposing fortress resisted all its sieges
until 1794 when it was taken by the troops of Agha Mohammed.

50

In the Dasht e Lut desert,
violent winds sometimes blow for weeks on end, raising immense dust clouds.

A RETURN JOURNEY TO BANDAR ABBAS

The Polos arrived in the kingdom of Kerman. Kerman had become prosperous from its metal and precious stone working industries. The region was rich in turquoise mines, now depleted, and iron ore mines. Knights' armor, bridles and swords were made here. After loading up on provisions, our three Venetians left Kerman heading south towards Hormuz (present-day Bandar Abbas), on the Persian Gulf. Located directly opposite the Straits of Hormuz, the city already had a prominent strategic and economic role. From there they intended to take the maritime route. For seven days they crossed a "very great plain [...] very hot." It was a beautiful region and seemed quite prosperous. Marco saw great quantities of fruit trees, citrus trees, and large herds of sheep and oxen, but he also noticed in these pleasant oases "several cities, market towns and villages with earthen walls of great height and thickness to protect them against their enemy, a people named the Karaunas, who infest the country, a cruel and evil race of marauders who run rampant across the country doing great harm." Moreover, the Polo's caravan came up against them and only by luck did they manage to extricate themselves.

The region has kept both its agricultural prosperity and its bad reputation. Even today foreigners are advised not to travel the Bandar Abbas road at night. Although there may still be the odd highwayman, there is no comparison with the situation Marco Polo described.

Desert trails leading to the north and east
come to the occasional oasis,
often dominated by a traditional watchtower.

When our travelers got to Hormuz, they found a city with a stifling climate tucked away below its date palm trees. The city and its great port were teeming with European, Arab and Indian merchants. There were spices, silk and golden fabrics, precious woods, pearls and elephant trunks in abundance. The inhabitants were dark-skinned and avoided working out of doors during the heat of the summer.

Here again, what the Polos saw and what one can see today differ little. Bandar Abbas is still a hot, dirty, overcrowded metropolis. A great amount of maritime trade continues to transit through its port which is cluttered with cranes and containers. Many ships from Europe and Asia dock daily or put out to sea. Owing to the unstable political situation in the region, the military port houses numerous warships. This atmosphere is reflected by the colorful mixed population which although it resembles that of all the great tropical ports, knows that it is sitting on a powder keg.

For some reason that Marco does not give in *Description of the World*, the Polos suddenly decided to return to Kerman. Perhaps they had heard of the war that was blocking most of the ports in southern China. They were, no doubt, also put off by the poor state of the "bad, fragile and dangerous" ships on which they were to continue their journey.

In the small oases close to the Afghan border,
far from the major routes
and the political fervor and strife of Teheran,
life continues to flow by peaceably.

The population of the remote areas have kept most of their customs.
Two typical examples are a cook from Kuhbonan and a silversmith from Zahedan, using a blowpipe.

HEADING TOWARDS AFGHANISTAN

After a seven-day journey on horseback over a difficult track through a moon-like landscape, Marco Polo and his companions reached the city of Kuh-banan (present-day Kuhbonan). They had crossed the center of the terrible Dasht-e Lut the most inhospitable of the Iranian deserts. As today, only the rare semi-nomadic tribe with its transhumant livestock live there, constantly on the move in search of new pasturage. Paradoxically, it is among these very traditional micro-societies that the militant Islam of the Teheran ayatollahs has had the least impact.

As he was turning east around Khorassan, Marco heard of the strange story of the Old Man of the Mountain and his Assassins. According to legend, which has indeed been partially confirmed by historical fact, an important Ismaelite master (there were in fact a long line of them from 1090 to 1255) from the region of Alamut in central Iran, had founded a sect of fanatic Muslims. They were called "hashishin" or assassins, because they were given hashish to consume before being sent out on a mission. They killed those considered ungodly, having been promised future rewards of women, silver and hashish. This formidable sect had more than one murder to its credit, including that of a Shah of Persia, a grand vizier of Egypt and any number of Crusaders.

Carpet weavers
in a Khorassan workshop.
The labor force is often composed
of young children.

The little group of Polos continued wending its way northeastward. Northern Afghanistan, formerly Bactria, spread out before them. They soon discovered the beautiful city of Sheberghan (present-day Shibarghan), nestled in the heart of a fertile, green oasis. Unfortunately today's traveler is not so lucky. The city's appearance has greatly changed. Shibarghan, the capital of the Afghan province of Jozjan, is a polluted industrial center whose sole activities are related to the pipelines carrying gas to Russia. And even they have been interrupted for the past fifteen years by the bloody civil war.

The Venetians were now on the Silk Route. They reached Balkh on the border of the Lordship of Persia's empire. Completely fallen into oblivion today, Balkh was once an

important crossroads for the various branches of the Silk Route. They went on to Gana and Talikan (Khanabad and Taloqan). What Marco saw on the outskirts of these two cities was certainly not very different from what one sees today, excepting, of course, the effects of the war. *Description of the World* says, "There is a large market for wheat and other grains [...] the mountains face south [...] some are entirely of tasty white salt and hard as stone. Men come from all the surrounding country, making a thirty-day journey to fetch this salt, which is the best in the world." The markets, particularly the livestock market, still exist. Political conditions permitting, asses still transport rock salt from the mines located south of the city at the foot of those high somber mountains around which Marco Polo's caravan traveled.

In western Afghanistan the nomads are strict, but not fanatical, Muslims.
One can often see men proudly walking their dogs.
These mastiffs are used to protect the herds from wolves.

◁

Many refugees fled the center of the country
for makeshift camps near the Iranian border.

A Baluchi woman from Registan and a Pachto (or Pathan) woman from Kuh-e Bab.
The women stay in the tents doing the daily household chores.

▷

Wars have been devastating Afghanistan for the past twenty years,
but traditional markets continue to flourish as this one, near Taloqan.

Most of Afghanistan is a succession of narrow, very isolated valleys.
Only the men travel; along the way numerous restaurants provide their meals.

The Provinces of Badakhshan and Pashai

FROM NORTHERN AFGHANISTAN TO THE PAMIRS

*The Polos finally reached Scasem (present-day Ishkashim),
now a small mountain market town where numerous trails and mule tracks join together
after descending from the nearby mountains.
Marco and his companions enjoyed the fish from the mountain torrents;
braised trout is still one of the culinary specialties of the region.*

NORTHERN AFGHANISTAN

After three days' traveling, the Polos entered Afghan Badakhshan. They were now in the Amu Darya valley. This large Asian river, the Oxus of yore, has its source in the Pamirs and empties into the Aral Sea after meandering for 2,540 kilometers. It is the natural border between Afghanistan and Tadzhikistan. The Badakhshan region was renowned for its magnificent rubies. Even though they are no longer mined, the famous balas rubies that Marco Polo so admired there brought wealth to the province for many centuries. Until the civil war caused the mines to close, Afghan Badakhshan produced, in addition to rubies - sapphires, lapis-lazuli, silver, lead and copper. Moreover, neighboring Tadzhikistan, despite its internal problems, continues to extract these natural resources.

A Pachto war dance.
The Afghano-Pakistani border runs through the lands of these fierce warriors,
but neither country can control the territory.

Pure mountain air is considered to be the best remedy for all sorts of illnesses and Marco Polo's experience seems to confirm this. "While he was in those regions, Messer Marco was ill for about a year and as soon as he went to the mountains, he felt better again."

Once he was restored to health, the little troop set out again. The Polos were now at the entrance to the Wakhan corridor. They started into the relatively low, narrow strip of land pointing from northeast Afghanistan towards the Pamir, Hindu Kush and Kashmiri highlands, the only natural way into Chinese Xinjiang, where the main branch of the Silk Route ran.

Most of the northeastern territories are under tribal administration.
Because of the many long-standing rivalries between clans,
each extended family possesses a fortified house.

Northern Afghanistan and Pakistan
were the seat of the brilliant Greco-Buddhist civilization of Gandhara
which flourished between the first and fifth centuries.
The remains of the past blend harmoniously with modern constructions built in a traditional manner.

As one approaches the Wakhan corridor
there is a change in the physical features of the people.
Authentic Indo-Europeans live side by side
with mixed Asian and Altaic populations.

The dromedary is the principal means of transport in the desert plains,
but donkeys are widely used for work in the fields because they are agile and easy to keep.

Farmed terraces cover the valley slopes of the many rivers
(Amu Darya, Piandj, Kunar ...) and their tributaries.

The determination
of the Afghan people is visible
on the face of this man
from Wakhan.

In the springtime shepherds drive the immense herds of sheep up to high mountain pastures,
then move them down again at the beginning of autumn.

KAFIRISTAN

At this point in the journey, Marco Polo mentions the mysterious province of Pashai, located in southern Badakhshan. It is in fact Kafiristan, known to the Afghan Muslims as Nuristan. Speaking of the inhabitants of this area which was already known for its cultural identity and its voluntary isolation, Marco Polo described them as "idolaters, idol worshipers [...]. They know many enchantments and diabolic arts and they spend their time invoking demons." In a region divided between Buddhist and Muslim influences, the persistence of strange and rather contrasting cultures could only result in the inhabitants of Nuristan being labeled heretics. In the nineteenth century they were massacred by a fanatical Muslim leader. The survivors had to convert to Islam, while some preferred to flee to Pakistan. Settled on the eastern slopes of the Hindu Kush, their descendants have managed to preserve their surprising culture in Pakistani Kafiristan, literally, the "Land of the Pagans." Indeed, a very ancient type of Hellenistic tradition has been perpetuated here, giving birth to the Kalash culture. In three isolated valleys this blue-eyed people has preserved a culture dating back to the period of Alexander the Great from whom they claim to be descended. There are only three thousand survivors left, trying to resist as best they can the persecutions of ubiquitous Islam.

Considered second-class citizens, they are slowly wilting under the pressure of forced acculturation and different types of harassment.

The Amu Darya basin and those of its tributaries form the border between Tadzhikistan and northern Afghanistan.
Here Marco Polo saw the balas rubies for which the region is so renowned.

◁

Few families send their children to school.
Here the Koran provides the basic education.

In the Hindu Kush foothills,
sheep and goat raising is the basis of the economy.

Except for the bottomlands, the hostile relief makes farming practically impossible.
Century-old terraces exploit every available bit of land.

A young woman from the village of Brun, wearing a shushut. The different types of women's headdresses indicate the clan, the social status and the wealth of the owner's family.

*The Kalash live in three valleys of the eastern Hindu Kush :
the Birir, the Bumboret and the Rumbur. Considered impure pagans by other Pakistanis,
the Kalash continue to practice pre-Islamic rituals.*

The men wear this traditional hat,
typical of Pakistan
and northern Afghanistan.
The flowers, leaves
or colored feathers differentiate them
from Muslims.

Modern Kalash life is unchanged from that of their ancestors.
This woman from Rumbur is cooking a barley flatbread using flour
from a mill operated by a couple from Birir.

*The first snow-capped peaks of the Karakorum chain
stand out beyond the foothills of northern Kashmir.*

THE NORTHWESTERN REACHES OF KASHMIR

Did Marco Polo really go to Kashmir? His observations in *Description of the World*, albeit precise, do not offer a positive answer. The Venetian may have gathered information from other travelers or merchants. It does seem however, that he made a detour to the south to visit some valleys that could be reached "by many woods, deserts and such narrow and steep mountain passes." Unfortunately in the twentieth century the province of Kashmir is at war, torn between Pakistan and India which have been fighting for its possession since 1947. Most of the population is Muslim. In Marco Polo's time it was a happy region. The Buddhist inhabitants divided their time between farming and hunting. Marco was struck by the great number of monasteries and hermitages he found there. In the course of conflicts and invasions they were all destroyed. He also mentioned the beautiful complexion of the inhabitants. "The Kashmiri men are generally brown-skinned and thin. The women are really beautiful for dark-complexioned people" Although this last remark lacks tact, it does reveal the Kashmiri

The northern course of the Indus and its tributaries pass through arid regions populated mainly by Buddhist Tibetans.

women's reputation for beauty. From the great Mogul emperor Akbar, who used to come here to rest and to choose his new wives, to the modern visitor to these high valleys, everyone admires the distinguished looks and fine features of the women.

One of the many Koranic schools in Ladakh.
Conversions to Islam have increased among the Buddhist population.
The boys have uniforms and the girls must wear a scarf.

The climatic conditions are extremely varied.
Whereas the highlands have a cold dry continental climate,
the valleys enjoy temperate weather.

Thanks to this complex system of canals,
Kashmir has come to be known as "the Venice of the Orient."

*The dark brown hair and blue eyes
of this highlander denote
his Indo-Aryan origin, with obvious
Caucasian predominance.*

*For centuries nomads have crossed the Himalayan foothills
looking for pastures for their herds.
The conflict between India and Pakistan has profoundly disturbed their way of life.*

The Shyok valley in autumn. The level of the Kaberi and Kondus range runoff is beginning to go down, revealing large sand banks.

BALTISTAN

As one ascends the valley of the Wakhan, a tributary of the Amu Darya, the dense mass of the Pamirs rises to the left. The Polo caravan followed the course of the river *Description of the World* calls "the great river of Badakhshan." Here they were face to face with a wild monumental environment of disproportionate, breath-taking grandeur. Marco wrote "we are almost always crossing mountains; the peaks are so high that at every summit we say this is the highest in the world." Although the Pamir chain may not be the highest, it culminates at 7,7199 meters and its average altitude is around 5,000 meters. The numerous alpine pastures are rich and perfect for sheep and cattle raising. Here one first encounters Himalayan yaks.

For forty days the Venetians' caravan continued wending its way eastward. "There are no homes, nor inns [...] this country is known as Belor. The people are scattered among the high

*Baltistan got its name
from the predominant ethnic group, the Balti.
The population is poor and tries to scrape a living
from infertile soil.*

mountains. They are idolatrous and very wild." The region described by Marco Polo now goes by the name of Baltistan. This back-country province is difficult to reach and extends from Gilgit to Kashmir. Five torrential rivers, all of them tributaries of the Indus, dig gashes in the high mountains, forming enormous blocks. Deep in the narrow valleys, along the steep banks, the occasional small terraced field affords subsistence agriculture.

For many years the province was part of Buddhist Tibet. In fact, until the sixteenth century when the Muslims conquered it, it was known as little Tibet. The population is of obvious Tibetan origin that has more recently mixed with Indo-European and Mongol blood. Even at the end of the twentieth century, Baltistan remains one of the most pristine regions of the Karakorum, in the western Himalayas.

The mountain people of Baltistan
are isolated in their high valleys.
Formerly Buddhists, they converted
to Shiite Islam
in the sixteenth century.

*The Balti cross rivers
on zakhts (rafts supported
by inflated goat skins)
as did their ancestors
over two thousand years ago.*

*The influence of the Gandhara culture was felt as far as Baltistan.
Although the Silk Route did not penetrate into this region,
many Buddhist monuments can be found at the ends of the main valleys.*

The sedentary Uighurs are surrounded by many nomad tribes.
The Kazakhs to the north and the Kirghiz to the east and the south
are the two largest non-Uighur groups in western Xinjiang.

Another minority, the Tadzhiks,
live in the southwestern part
of the country.
Although they are few
in number, they play an important
role in the political life of the region.

The Pamir range in a violent spring storm.

The ruins of the Taxhorgan fortress overlooking the village of the same name.
It was once a prosperous city, one of the most important halting places on the Silk Route.

Market day in Kashgar.
The narrow streets cannot accommodate heavy traffic and carts must be left at the entrance to the city.

▷

A typical example of religious architecture in western Xinjiang,
with the elegant, brightly-colored minarets.

An old Uighur peasant
has come to Kashgar
to sell his produce.

The Kingdom of Kashgar
WESTERN XINJIANG

*Just like any modern visitor leaving the Pamirs,
Marco Polo received a shock on discovering Chinese Turkestan, which has now become the autonomous province
of Xinjiang. As he followed the narrow road winding through the sumptuous landscape
he was fascinated by the high plateau sloping gently down towards the arid expanses of western Xinjiang.
The Polos' expedition entered what in the West was then called Great Turkey.*

KASHGAR : THE CITY AND THE PROVINCE.

Despite the lack of precision in *Description of
the World*, their small group probably went through the city of Taxhorgan, a major halting place
on the caravan trails. Today, on visiting this small, forgotten market-town, one can hardly
restrain a nostalgic thought of what had once been one of the most crowded crossroads of the
Silk Route. The Polos' trail can be found a little farther along, where the high valleys wind their
way between enormous chunks of stone mountains.

They were headed towards the Kashgar plain. The kingdom of Kashgar corresponded to the
present region of Kashgar in the autonomous Chinese region of Xinjiang. Marco noted the
intense activity of the traders that took place there. Local prosperity resulted from its
favorable location at the junction of the Silk Route's main branches. The inhabitants were

*Kashgar, known by the Chinese as Kashi,
is still the active, busy trading center it was
in Marco Polo's times, although the Silk Route
has long since disappeared.*

*Sunday is bazaar day.
All the stalls are open,
ready for thousands of villagers
from the surrounding countryside.*

*Bazaar day is also a time
for getting together with friends
and for bargaining of all sorts.*

*The men of Kashgar are accustomed
to having their early morning coffee
in a neighborhood restaurant.*

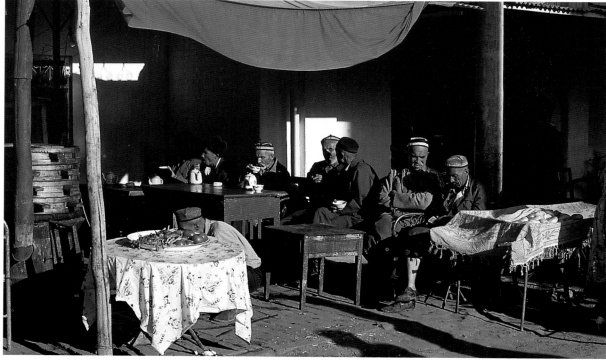

already Mohammedans. Marco recorded that "many goods and clothes arrive here. The inhabitants earn their living as artisans and traders [...]. Many merchants set out to market their wares throughout the world." He also pointed out the agricultura! wealth of the region, with its cotton, hemp and flax crops, and its many vineyards and orchards.

Kashgar is called Kashi by the Chinese. Although the silk trade has long since ended, quantities of merchandise from central Asia, especially from Tashkent and Alma Ata, still enter China via Kashgar. After the Second World War it became one of western Xinjiang's important agricultural and business centers, and today the city is the political and cultural capital of the Uighurs.

The harmonious mixture of Western, Turkish and Chinese styles
is visible in the architecture.

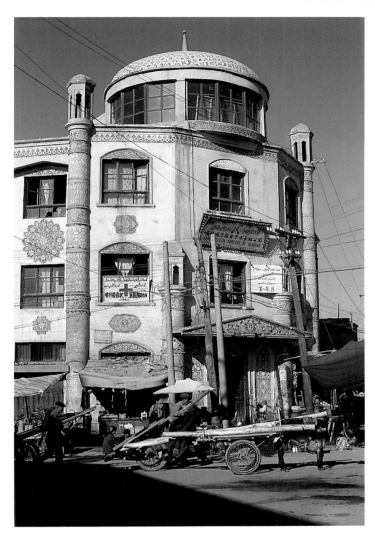 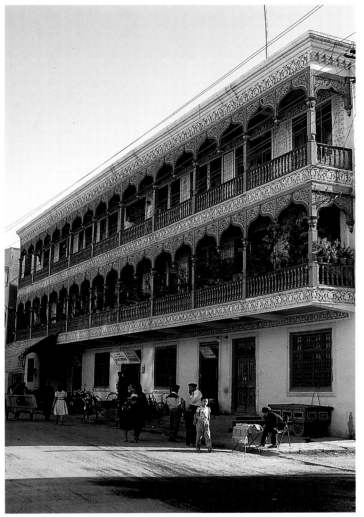

Traditional medicine and medicinal preparations,
including exorcisms and potions obtained from plants and animals,
are held in high esteem among the population.

THE UIGHURS

Nearly seventy per cent of the population of western Xinjiang are Uighurs. This people of Turkic origin constitutes a relatively homogeneous group, despite a mingling of its Altaic roots with Mongol and Indo-European blood over the course of the centuries. They settled here around the ninth century, chasing out the early Indo-Europeans, though certain traces of the original stock show through in the faces of some people from the north. Islam arrived in their lands as early as 900 A.D. For four centuries the Uighurs resisted the sirens of the new religion, preserving their Manichean rites and their Nestorian or Buddhist faiths. It is during this period that Marco Polo encountered them. At the beginning of the fourteenth century, however, the great Uighur leaders were either bribed or convinced by the Arabs and one after the other they converted to Islam. They then set up a society governed by the strict morals of an inflexible religion. They also fought fiercely against all attempts to conquer them. It was only during the Sino-Manchurian reconquest in the eighteenth century that Kashgar became Xinjiang, literally "the New Step" of China. Today, the Uighurs number

An encampment of yurts in southern Xinjaing.
This is the base camp for caravans about to cross the nearby mountains.

Yurts of a Kazakh group during autumn.
A piece of felt closes the tops of the tents as well as the entrance door in order to keep in the heat.

A traditional tent should be able to provide shelter for the entire family.
At night, partitions of material are put in place to provide privacy for couples and children.

*During the summer, the yurt door is thrown open
and the piece of felt or hide used to seal the roof is removed.*

*Carpet making, the great specialty
of all the peoples of central Asia,
takes up much of the women's time.
They also know how to prepare
koumiss, a succulent drink
of fermented mare's milk.*

over eighteen million. Their community, with its distinctive political and cultural features, is regularly shaken by strong autonomist, even secessionist, movements. Beijing has good reason to worry : the proximity of other Turkish-speaking peoples of central Asia - the Kirghizes, the Kazakhs, the Uzbek, the Tadzhik and the Turkmens - who are themselves tempted by the collapse of the Soviet block ; the strategic and economic importance of the Uighur territory which is located at the opening of the great India-Pakistani corridors, as well as the far from discrete maneuvers of Turkey to unite under its banner the Turkish-speaking populations of central Asia are reason enough. National sovereignty is a touchy subject for the Chinese army. At this time it does not seem amenable to talk of dissidence. In the long run, the accumulation of all these factors can only lead to an explosive situation.

People suffering from rheumatism take baths of burning hot sand on the slopes of an immense dune
whose virtues have been known for centuries.

The physical appearance and way of life of the Uighurs
show a close resemblance to those of the Turks of the same Altaic ethno-cultural group.

Respect for tradition and a moderate form of Islam
are the two pillars of Muslim society in Xinjiang.

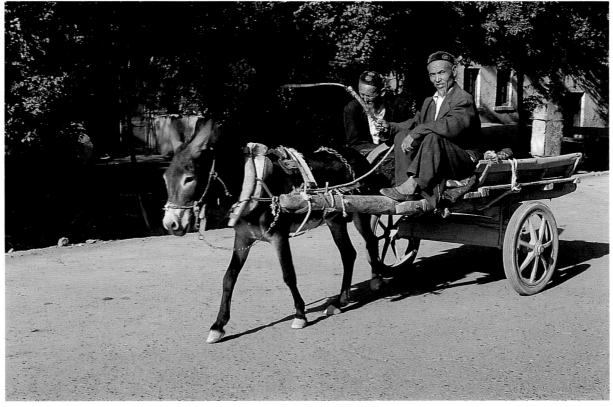

THE GREAT TAKLAMAKAN DESERT

The nomads who move around its outer limits call it "the desert of all deserts." Two long mountain ranges, the Tian Shan and the Kunlun, divide Xinjiang into three distinct zones : the Dzungaria basin to the north, where the Kazakhs live, the Taklamakan desert in the center, and the Tibetan high plateau in the south. The Taklamakan desert alone covers 370,000 square kilometers. It is one of the most desolate deserts in the world. Only the occasional thorn bush provides feed for the nomads' camel herds. After leaving Kashgar, Marco Polo decided to take the southern branch of the Silk Route. He followed the southern edge of the formidable desert for nearly two weeks. His route took the shape of an arc through Yarkan, Khotan, Pem to Charchan (present-day Yarkand, Hotan, Pem and Qiemo) in Xinjiang. It was a hard trial for the men and the animals. While they were enjoying a well-earned rest in Charchan, Marco noted the emotions the immensity of the Taklamakan had aroused in him: "All this province is of sand; from Khotan to Pem it is also sand, and from Pem to here it is even more sand; this is why there is so much bitter, bad water [...]. The

Last minute preparations for members of a caravan setting off toward the Pamir and Tian Shan Mountains.
The considerable caravan trade and the equally profitable countraband follow many trails,
some portions of which date back to the Silk Route.

prevailing wind is from the southwest and it immediately wipes out all footprints, covering them with sand."

The modern route avoids the desert. It runs a little further south than the trail the Polos' caravan took. Whoever absolutely wants to follow in their footsteps has to cross the southern part of the desert.

The remains of the city of Pem mentioned in *Description of the World* lie near a site known as Laodamagu, and the province of Charchan was probably the region between Yutian and Ruoqiang, that is, the areas within the lower boundaries of the Taklamakan. There, the contemporary traveler can understand what the word "desert" truly means !

No one dares to cross the Taklamakan desert.
The rare caravan follows trails along its edge.

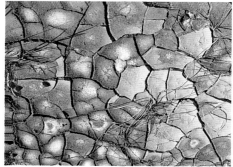

The Gobi desert is one of the most arid of the planet.
It hardly ever rains here.
And yet, thanks to the Silk Route,
important civilizations developed along its border.
Everywhere, ruins and tombs bear witness to this glorious past.

The Province of Tangut
FROM WESTERN XINJIANG TO INNER MONGOLIA

*After loading up on provisions,
the Venetians' caravan left Charchan. They traveled eastwards for five days when they came upon another desert,
at first glance even vaster than the Taklamakan. "This desert," says Marco, "is so long [...] one year is not enough
to reach the end of it; and at the narrowest point one struggles for a good month [...].
It consists entirely of mountains and plains of sand and valleys [...] and there is nothing to eat."*

THE GOBI DESERT

This desert used to be called the Lop, as did the long vanished city located at its entrance. It was, in fact, the Gobi Desert, stretching from northern China to Mongolia. The extreme climatic conditions there explain why, among the great deserts of the world, the Gobi is advancing the fastest each year. Our thirteenth century traveler was struck more by its hostile appearance than its wild beauty. He was especially sensitive to the strange legends of evil spirits that were, and still are, said to wander around day and night. The semi-nomads living on its outskirts and the nomads who occasionally cross the Gobi believe it to be a magical place where one must not venture without being on the lookout for ghosts and malevolent forces that disorient and lead the wayfarer astray, driving him crazy eventually to die of thirst.

Camels that used to carry merchandise
have become today's "taxis".

A young Tangut boy
from Yumenguan. He is of obvious
Tibeto-Burman origin.

When it rains the desert is covered with plants that eventually disappear, burnt dry by the sun.
Only thorn bushes can survive.

A view of the desolate expanse of the Gobi Desert
at the foot of the snow-capped Qilian Mountains.

Almost fifteen centuries ago the Manichaens built cave sanctuaries along the rivers that wind their way near the Burning Mountain (so called because of its red rocks).

DEAD CITIES OF THE NORTH AND TANGUT COUNTRY

After leaving the Lop, the Polos headed northeast once again. They followed the northern branch of the Silk Route which skirted the Tian Shan Mountains. They enter a region which is, from an archeological point of view, the richest in northern China. Opulent trading centers could be found side by side with cities which even then were in ruins, as well as with necropolises dating from the beginning of the Christian era. Certain large cities, such as Turfan and Hami, have survived and prospered. The entire area offers modern historians and archeologists an immense field for investigation, such is the wealth of the historical vestiges

As was his custom, in *Description of the World* Marco mentions regions that he himself probably never visited, but that his father and uncle had seen during their first trip. Such was the case for the kingdom of Kamul (present-day Hami) whose unusual, traditional way of offering hospitality to visitors Marco waggishly relates. Indeed, the men offered their wives and daughters to the passing visitor for the night. "The stranger stays in the house with the wife and does as he wishes, sleeping with her in a bed as if she were his wife and having a very good time at that !" Twentieth century travelers should not get their hopes up too high ; this custom disappeared a long time ago !

Various archeological digs have revealed
that the Bezeklik valley was inhabited by Manichaeans,
and then between the seventh and tenth centuries by Buddhists.
Only forty-odd painted caves still remain and even
those have been damaged by the weather, vandals and pillagers.

*Among the dead cities of the north,
the most famous is Jiaoche (or Yar or Yarkhoto).
It was the capital of the Xiongnu kingdom of Che Shi Qian
from 200 to 48 B.C., after which it came under Han domination.*

The Polos then entered the province of Tangut, approximately the equivalent of today's Gansu and Ningxia provinces. Strictly speaking, the Tangut were not a people, but rather a federation of Tibeto-Burman tribes. In 990 A.D. they founded a powerful kingdom which held sway over the whole central part of northern China until the thirteenth century, when Genghis Khan lay waste to their territory. Most of the twentieth century inhabitants of Gansu and Ningxia are descendants of the Tangut.

The main subject that excited Marco Polo's curiosity was his discovery of the true nature of asbestos. He was the first European to bring back precise information about "salamander," which was considered in the Middle Ages to be a magical substance. He revealed that it was not of animal origin, "neither beast nor serpent," but mineral and that it was extracted on the Xinjiang and Qinghai border. It is still mined today, mainly on the outskirts of the city of Mangnai. Here everything - houses, trees and crops - is covered with the whitish asbestos powder. Many residents wear face masks to avoid breathing in the omnipresent and ever so dangerous dust.

After the Hexi corridor comes the long desert plain
that runs along the northern side of the Qilian Mountains.
The traditional shape of the tombs indicates
an occasional Chinese Muslim graveyard.

Because of favorable climatic conditions, especially the heat,
this region has, since ancient times, furnished northern China with the best quality grapes.
Small villages emerge everywhere among the vineyards.

Religious Dunhuang

After thirty days on horseback, the Polos' caravan came to the great city of Sa-chau, present-day Dunhuang, in the heart of an attractive oasis. At the time, the inhabitants were Buddhists. A thousand grottos, filled with paintings, sculptures and reliefs, corresponding to the thousand Buddhas the fourth-century monk Lozun had seen in a vision, were dug into the face of an ochre cliff. Around it were thousands of monasteries and shrines. The inhabitants of the oasis were wealthy farmers. Despite his Christian bias, Marco Polo could not help being attracted to these peaceful Buddhists. He seems to have been particularly interested in the new year ritual festivities, along with the funeral custom of burning the dead, as is usual in Buddhist tradition. Soothsayers and other astrologers were extremely influential among the Tangut. Not only daily life, but also life after death, were governed by the oracles. Thus, noted Marco Polo, if their commandments are not respected, they threaten "that the evil spirits will hurt and kill certain members of the family. And as a result, the astrologers are obeyed word for word. For, were misfortune or an accident to befall any relative, or were he to perish, the astrologers would immediately say that it was the working of the spirit of death."

The heat is so intense during the summer (over fifty degrees Celsius)
that most homes have underground rooms.
*The ground floor serves as a terrace, protected by trellised vines or **toghrak**,*
called the "poplars of the Eurphrates".

The Dunhuang oasis, formerly an important halting place on the Silk Route, was a link between China and central Asia. Dunhuang alone, thanks to the great variety of its remains, is a summary of much of Chinese history. This pretty Mingsha shrine is hidden among high sand dunes surrounding the city.

The most beautiful landmark of Dunhuang is the famous Mogao cliff.
In the part open to the public there are 496 grottos containing almost 2,500 polychrome statues
and 45,000 square meters of paintings made between the fifth and the fourteenth centuries.

Surrounded by the Mongolian high plateaus to the north and the five-and-a half-thousand-meter Qilian Mountains to the south, the Dunhuang oasis closes the Hexi corridor. Historically and culturally the city has, since the late Middle Ages, been both a link and a barrier between the Hans' China and central Asia . Today, from all over the world, it attracts tourists eager to admire the wonders of the Mogao cliff. On the face of the 1,600 meter-long ochre cliff are two to four levels of the Thousand Buddha grottos. Only one hundred of the five hundred that remain can still be visited. Within them, however, there are still 2,500 statues, sculpted and painted between the fifth and the fourteenth centuries. Despite strict surveillance by the Chinese authorities, this enchanting sight allows both the amateur and the expert to imagine what Dunhuang was like in its heyday.

Mongol territories administered by the Chinese compose the autonomous region of Inner Mongolia.
This vast succession of steppes is over two and a half times the size of France.

Nomadism has given way to semi-nomadism.
Some Mongol encampments have symbolically kept the old yurt carts.
The sizes of the tents, now permanently attached to carts drawn by teams of oxen,
vary according to the social status of the owners.

SOUTH OF INNER MONGOLIA

The Polos continued on their way directly eastward. They crossed the province of Suggiu (present-day Suzhou in the province of Kansu) to reach the city of Kan-chau (present-day Ganzhou). For various reasons which Marco insists "are not worth mentioning" they remained there for over a year, to trade, it would seem. It is doubtless during this trip that the Venetian set out of visit the famous Tartars whom he had never seen. He traveled on to Etzina (present-day Ejinaqi), within the southern limits of Mongolia. Some commentators believe that this corresponds better to Kara-khoto, excavated from the sands in 1908 by the Russian Koslov. In either case, the city's importance rested on the fact that it was the rallying point for all caravans heading north towards Karakorum, Genghis Khan's former encampment. Ogodai, his successor, made it his capital.

Despite the description he gave, it is most unlikely that Marco Polo ever went there. However, excursions to the north of Etzina did introduce him to Mongol encampments. For the first time in his life, the young man found himself face to face with the Great Khan's warriors, those Buddhists the Pope had sent him to see.

The Mongol yurts are made of felt stretched over a low framework of poles and latticed panels.
Above them a bundle of willow sticks converge towards the hole in the roof which can be closed in cold weather.
White material, a symbol of good luck, often covers the outside of the yurt.

He suffered from the cold in the country where "the people are idolaters. They have camels and livestock in abundance [...]. And they live by agriculture and stock-rearing, not engaging in any trade." The remainder of this trip which he spent dancing attendance on Kubilai Khan, was to allow him to perfect his knowledge of Mongol customs, but he would never forget this first contact.

The visitor to Inner Mongolia today comes away with contrasting impressions. The few big cities are quite Chinese, whereas in the steppes the old Mongol way of life has been preserved. Winter is harsh and lasts almost nine months; summer is often windy and rainy. The landscape looks like a sea of close-cropped grass in the middle of which one perceives white yurts surrounded by large herds of horses. Formerly feared for their fighting spirit, the Mongols have become peaceful stock-raisers who still refuse stone or concrete dwellings. The men spend most of their time guarding the herds and making yurts, while the women are responsible for the daily chores, such as milking the cows, making butter, shearing the sheep and weaving clothes.

The skill of the expert Mongol horsemen has given them a worldwide reputation.
Their wild horse races across the steppes used to be synonymous with terror,
whereas today they provide an excuse for betting that often involves considerable sums of money.

*After leaving the western desert zones, the traveler reaches the great Chinese loess plateau
and enters a fertile region where green fields prevail over ochre hills.
Despite the harsh climate and the violent winds that dry the countryside, agriculture is rich and varied.
The region produces abundant crops of wheat, rice, cotton, millet, sorghum, melons and tobacco.*

▷

*Despite the vicissitudes of their eventful history, Ningxia and eastern Qinghai remain the regions of China
where Muslim influence is the greatest.*

The Provinces of Egrigaia and Tenduc

FROM NINGXIA TO BEIJING

As custom dictates, this woman is wearing a black veil on her small Muslim cap.

The Polos waited in Kan-chau for authorization from the Great Khan to advance farther into his lands. A military escort brought them Kubilai's order. The group left the city and once again set off on the Silk Route heading in a southeasterly direction. For five days they crossed an inhabited region where only "eerie spirits" murmured in the air. They arrived in Erguinl (present-day Lanzhou) on the eastern border of Tangut country.

LANZHOU AND THE MUSLIM ENCLAVES OF QINGHAI AND NINGXIA

At that time Lanzhou was an important caravan halting place, located on the south bank of the Yellow River. It had been the biggest city of western China since the sixth century, with a strong military garrison, and it controlled the Silk Route. Goods piled up in its warehouses.

In the twentieth century the city has become a great industrial center. Smoke and waste from the many petrochemical, nuclear and steel complexes pollute the air and inexorably corrode the monuments of yore. It is also one of the main railway junctions with innumerable trains chugging off towards Qinghai, Tibet, Ningxia, Outer Mongolia and Beijing.

On the Chinese scale, Ningxia is a small province. In protohistoric times it was, along with the eastern part of neighboring Qinghai province, long dominated by the Xia from the west.

Until the nineteenth century central Ningxia was home to several small Muslim kingdoms. They have managed to keep certain privileges, even today under the communist regime.

After having undergone various Chinese, Mongol and Manchu influences, these two regions of Buddhist tradition saw Islam impose its hegemony in the ninth century. The new religion progressed more rapidly here than elsewhere in China, giving birth to a number of small Muslim kingdoms. Despite the centuries-long rivalry among them, most of the Mohammedan principalities managed to survive into the early years of the twentieth century. The revolution of 1911 and the advent of the People's Republic in 1949, only slightly reduced their privileges. Eastern Qinghai and southern Ningxia in fact constitute semi-autonomous enclaves within the People's Republic.

Qinghai, a high plateau whose average altitude is about 2,300 meters, constitutes the eastern approach to Tibet. The two biggest Chinese rivers, the Yellow River and the Blue River, have their sources here. A majority of Tibetans has settled in the south, while Mongols and Kazakhs live in the north. Many of them are semi-nomads most of whose income is derived from livestock raising. The peoples living in the east have inter-married with the Hans and are almost all sedentary Muslims. The same type of population can be found in Ningxia, which is much greener and more agricultural than its neighbor.

We are certain that Marco Polo visited these lands while he was in Lanzhou, or later, during the missions that Kubilai entrusted to him. Yet, it is difficult to know exactly when and where.

Two typical sights of the region :
peasant women wearing the Islamic veil on their way to market
and a cook making pasta by the meter !

Description of the World, however, does specifically mention his visits to Egrigaia and Silingiu, present-day Yinchuan and Xining, the capitals of Ningxia and Qinghai, respectively. The composition of the population he described, "Nestorian Christians, idolaters and Mohametans," confirms what we know from other sources. If the Nestorians have since disappeared, the Buddhists are eminently present. Between Lanzhou and Xining one can visit the two superb lamaseries of Lhabrang and Ta'er Kumbum, centers of the Yellow Hat school of Buddhism. It is here that Marco Polo also saw yaks for the first time, those "wild oxen and cows, as big as elephants, and very handsome in appearance, for they are very hairy, except on their backs, and are black and white in color. Their coats are said to be extraordinary; their beautiful white wool is finer than silk."

The Muslim majority in this region has conserved most of its customs intact.
One of the most unusual ones is the cricket market. The insects are reputed to bring good luck and before making his choice,
the potential buyer will listen carefully to the song of each insect in its tiny cage.

THE GREAT WALL

Next, the Polos continued their way northeastward along the left bank of the Huanghe. They entered the province of Tenduc, a region in Inner Mongolia, just north of the bend in the river. One of the controversies concerning *Description of the World* is related to this episode : Marco believed he had located the wall of Gog and Magog in the province of Tenduc. One of the major questions raised by Marco Polo's book is that he never speaks explicitly about the Great Wall of China, although our thirteenth-century travelers could not have missed it. The route they took followed it for over one thousand kilometers. However surprising it may be, no mention is made of the Great Wall. Nor did Marco describe any of the monuments he inevitably must have seen along the way. The reasons for these omissions remain obscure. However, there appears to be a clear reference to the Great Wall in the chapter devoted to the province of Tenduc. At that time, the region was inhabited

by the Oengut, a tribe of Turkish origin. In his wish to see everything in terms of the Bible, the Venetian did not hesitate to recognize in the Mongols and the Oengut, the Magogs and Gogs of the Old testament, two peoples who were supposed to inhabit the Northeast of the Earth and who, according to tradition, were to spread the wrath of God at the end of time. So, since the Mongols and the Oengut, many of whom were Nestorians, therefore Christians, had undertaken to attack the Muslims, the affair was settled for Marco Polo; here were the biblical Gogs and Magogs ! The Koran offered important additional information. It mentioned a very ancient myth according to which Alexander the Great had constructed long walls and gigantic iron gates to separate the civilized world from Yadjoudj and Madjouj. Like the Arab travelers of previous centuries, Marco Polo again identified Gog and Magog. For him, the Great Wall of China and the walls of Alexander the Great were, in fact, one and the same !

The remains of the Great Wall follow ancient trails.
The vast expanses of steppe stretching to the north are ample explanation
why the wall was constructed by the Middle Empire as protection against
the incessant barbarian invasions from Mongolia.

THE GREAT KHAN AND MARCO

The Polos began the last leg of the journey that was to lead them to the Great Khan. The caravan first went through the merchant town of Sindaciu (present-day Xuanhua in the Hebei province). It went on to the area of Chagan-nor, present-day Tchaghan'nor or the Mongols' "Blue Lake" where Kubilai Khan owned a sumptuous hunting palace. Three days later the caravan reached the city of Chandu (present-day Shang-tu), sometimes called Chemeinfu in *Description of the World*. It had been the Great Khans' summer capital since the twelfth century.

It was now the summer of 1275. The lord of Cathay (ie., northern China), Kubilai, Great Khan of all the Tartars, son of Tului "the Mirror," grandson of Genghis Khan "prince of the Ocean," welcomed the Venetian travelers with every honor. Niccolo and Maffeo told him the

results of their mission. They were far from what he had anticipated, as the one hundred wise men he had requested of the Pope had not come. He nevertheless happily accepted the papal credentials and the holy oil from the lamp in Christ's Sepulcher presented to him in the Pope's name. The Tartar monarch then noticed the comely appearance of young Marco. He was now twenty-one years old. A teen-ager at the start, he had been seasoned by the rigors of the voyage. *Description of the World* provides some light on this turning point in young Marco Polo's life. "When the Great Khan saw Marco, who was a young gentleman, he asked who he was. Sire, said Messer Niccolo, he is my son and your servant [...]. Let him be welcome for he pleases me greatly," said the Great Khan. Marco Polo had seduced the Mongol sovereign. The life of the young Venetian was to take a totally unexpected turn.

1276 - 1291
In the Great Khan's Service

arco Polo was undeniably

a talented young man and could but have pleased Kubilai.

The Venetian spoke and wrote at least four languages, Arabic, Turkish, Persian and Mongol,

whose rudiments his father and uncle had taught him during their travels.

Like most of the Mongols, moreover, he most certainly knew no Chinese.

At first the sovereign brought him to court ceremonies and festivities;

then he initiated him into the arcana of power and the Mongol administration.

He was soon ready to be of use to the Khan. Marco became a sort of imperial tax inspector.

Several times, the Great Khan commissioned him to verify tax collections in the far-away provinces of the southwest

and the southeast, including Kinsai (present-day Hangzhou) and especially Yangui (present-day Yangzhou)

where he was governor for three years.

From here on **Description of the World** contents itself with the presentation of Marco Polo's various missions.

No further mention is made of his uncle or his father,

except to indicate that they continued to trade whenever the opportunity arose.

The Province of Cathay
FROM BEIJING TO EASTERN SICHUAN

Two examples of historical treasures in Beijing :
the animals that guard the Mings' tomb
and the stairway leading to the Halls
of Perfect Harmony and Supreme Harmony.

Present-day Beijing then went by the name of Cambalu,
in Mongol, Khan-balik or "city of the Khan." Sometimes it was called Dadu.
One million two hundred thousand people lived in what was already the biggest city on earth.
The Polos' stay in Cambalu coincided with a period of great political and military activity.
Kubilai was completing two major enterprises.
He was finishing the unification of northern China, known in Europe as Cathay.
To the south he was trying, once and for all, to subjugate the Sungs who had founded the empire Marco called Manzi.

THE BEIJING MEGALOPOLIS

Cambalu was the capital of Cathay. It was surrounded by a wall forty kilometers in circumference. Regularly laid out quarters and rationally planned streets were a far cry from anything Marco Polo had seen before. The young man described with a profusion of details the palaces of the Great Kahn and his sons. The imperial palace where the sovereign stayed from December to February was located at the center of a veritable aristocratic city, surrounded by a double high-walled enceinte. There was considerable wealth within. "The palace is so large, so beautiful, so rich and so well arranged that there cannot be in this world a man able to imagine or to make something finer," wrote Marco admiringly.

133

The great courtroom in the Imperial Palace of the Forbidden City. For the Chinese it was at the center of the known world.
They called it the "violet - purple - forbidden - city" by analogy with the colors of the north star
which was considered to be the center of the cosmos.

He was constantly amazed at the uninterrupted flow of merchants entering and leaving the twelve gates of the city. "To my mind there is not a city in the world to which so many merchants come, where such great quantities of precious, valuable things arrive - gems, pearls, silk and spices." The population was very cosmopolitan. Mixed with the Chinese were Mongols, Turks, Persians, Arabs and various peoples of central Asia. The Mongols and the wealthiest families from the other communities resided in the center of Cambalu, not far from the imperial city in what was called the "inner city." Even noble Chinese were refused entry, with rare exceptions. They had to live outside the walls, near the common people, crowded into the Chinese town known as the "outer city," or in the outlying neighborhoods or in any one of the two hundred satellite towns which, according to Marco Polo, formed the suburbs of the great capital. Modern Beijing has conserved very little of ancient Cambalu. After the Yuans, it remained the capital of China and was given its current name which means the "northern capital." In the fifteenth century, the almost deified Ming rulers had the Forbidden City built on the perimeter of the former Tartar

city; here they could live hidden from the eyes of the common people. In the twentieth century the capital has been deeply perturbed by a succession of upheavals : the revolution of 1911, the stormy departure of the last emperor, Pu Yi, in 1924, and most significantly, Communist control under Mao Zedong since 1949 and in particular, the bloody Cultural Revolution of 1966. Everything that evoked imperial power was fought, destroyed or transformed. The ramparts, the great gates, the "pailou" or porticos at the crossroads and most of the temples and monasteries were leveled. Thus, except for the Forbidden City which, although totally depersonalized, has become a tourist must, and some temples and historical edifices that miraculously escaped Communist uniformalization, Beijing is now a cold, impersonal city. Wide avenues cut through anonymous gray blocks of austere buildings. In general, the architecture reminds one of the defunct Soviet Union.

Cars remain a luxury of the privileged few : most of the thirteen million inhabitants ride bicycles, silently meeting and passing each other in compact swarms.

◁

*Lake Kunming and the various lesser artificial lakes
and ponds take up more than three-quarters of the Summer Palace's two hundred and ninety hectares.
Construction of the palace began in the thirteenth century.
During the following centuries it was constantly altered.
In 1860 Franco-British troops lay sack to it.
In 1888, Empress Cixi (Tseu Hsi) had it rebuilt.*

*As early as the twelfth century the Beijing rulers chose to set up summer residences northwest of the city,
in the Yanshan and Taihang piedmonts, constructing numerous small palaces, pavilions and kiosks.
It is rather the parks they built, however, that still lend charm to the area.
To the west of the Summer Palace in the foothills of the Miafeng mountains,
lie the famous Perfumed Hills with their superb gardens and ornamental lakes.*

137

General view of the Buddhist cave temples in Yun Gang.
All of the fifty-three caves were sculptured during the second half of the fifth century under Pei Wei rule.

SEVERAL VOYAGES IN ONE

Description of the World tells us that the Great Khan entrusted Marco with a mission to southwest China, more precisely "towards the west in a far-away land, to a city called Karajang." The report adds that after accounting for his mission to the complete satisfaction of Great Khan, "he stayed with the Great Khan fully seventeen years; and in all this time he never ceased to be sent on missions." Marco Polo did not feel it necessary to supply us with other particulars of his many journeys, limiting himself to describe in detail, his trip to Karajang, or "the black kingdom." This name designates a non-Chinese kingdom in the northern part of Yunnan conquered by Kubilai in 1253. In fact, the stages of this trip, as it is recounted in *Description of the World*, represent a synthesis of several missions conducted in the region. However, out of respect for Marco Polo's wishes, we shall consider that it was, indeed, one single voyage.

The originality of Yungang lies
in the successful syncretism between Chinese,
Indian, Irano-Sassanian, Hellenistic
and central Asian art styles.

A colossal statue of Maitreya, the Buddha of the Future,
surrounded by the Thousand Buddhas.

*The suspended monastery of Xuankong, near the village of Hunyan,
on the side of a cliff facing Mount Hengshan, one of the five sacred peaks in China.
It is famous for its wooden building, tiled roofs and paintings.
It was constructed under the Pei Wei in the fifth century and altered under the Qing in the seventeenth century.*

FROM YONGDING TO THE YELLOW RIVER

After a four-month journey across Cathay, Marco saw the great river Pulisanghin, whose name meant "stone bridge" for the very large bridge across the Yongding, known today as "Marco Polo's bridge." Numerous junks follow it down to the sea. He then moved on to the rich province of Hebei where he visited the city of Chou-chau (present-day Zhuoxian), famous for it woven silk fabrics. Making his way southwest he then arrived in Shanxi, which he called the kingdom of Taianfu. Shanxi is located in the eastern part of the great slate plateau of northern China. Its western facade follows the course of the Huanghe and it appears to be a sort of natural fortification between Mongolia and the plains to the south.

In the thirteenth century, the Venetian was pleasantly surprised by the beauty and the fertility of the countryside, as well as the hospitality of the people, so unlike the natural reserve of the Hans under Mongol domination. He wrote that one found "many beautiful towns and villages, much trade and activity, highly cultivated, handsome fields producing quantities of silk, grapevines and trees. The people are sedentary, wealthy and friendly." The province's main activity is still farming, with crops of millet, gaoliang, wheat and corn.

The substratum abounds in ores. Two-thirds of the Chinese coal production comes from Shanxi. It is the center of the powerful iron and textile industries, the latter a carry-over from Marco Polo's times.

*Ningxia, Hebei and Shanxi (Tainanfu to Marco Polo) have certain remarkable archeological remains,
some of which date back to the neolithic age.*

Taoism is still deeply rooted among the country folk. The proliferation of pagodas are there to remind one that Mao Zedong's Cultural Revolution was unable to eradicate the way of Tao.

Like their ancestors three thousand years ago, the riverside residents of the Huanghe continue to cross the water on small rafts supported by inflated goatskins.

SOUTH OF THE YELLOW RIVER

The Venetian then crossed "a river called Kara-moran, which is so wide and so deep a bridge cannot span it." This was the Huanghe, the Yellow River, known as Qaramuren, or the "Black River" in Mongol; he crossed it on large platforms built for that purpose. Next, he headed westward to reach "the noble city of Cacianfu," which historians have been unable to identify. He then proceeded up the Wei valley riding horseback for about eight days to enter the present-day province of Shaanxi. At the end of the road rose "the beautiful, vast city of Singan-fu (present-day Xi'an). It was the ancient capital of the Qins, the city of the first Chinese emperor Qin Shi Huangdi. The city housed many historical monuments. Marco was particularly impressed with the large castle belonging to the lord of Mangalai, one of Kubilai's sons. This magnificent structure was built on the outskirts of the city. Marco gave a full description of the power and originality of its architecture and the luxury and grandeur of the various rooms. Unfortunately, modern Xi'an, now an important industrial and farming center, has hardly kept any vestiges of its prestigious past, except for a series of tombs. In 1974 it came to worldwide renown when farmers digging a well not far from Qin Shi Huangdi's grave discovered slightly taller than life-sized terra cotta figures five meters underground. The archeologists who were called in unearthed a fabulous army of seven thousand soldiers, foot soldiers, horsemen, chariot drivers, all in battle order, lined up in 230-meter-long corridors. All of them dated back to the third century B.C. It was Qin Shi Huangdi's army. The monarch had wanted it to accompany him even to his death !
But, of course, Marco Polo knew nothing of this.

The Yellow River is nicknamed the "Sorrow of China"
because of the color given to its waters by silt carried down from the Ordos plateau.
The middle course of the river loops around what is the largest loess plateau in the world.

The upper and middle reaches of the Huanghe often flow through sandy banks.
The Tengger desert is the last arid zone in the south; beyond it lie great expanses of fertile land.

The style and rhythm of life have not changed in centuries.
One can still find adobe houses and large collective beds heated by wood furnaces
that were described in ancient texts.

Celestial guardians on the wall of Ju Xian Si.
They are part of the complex of Long Men caves.
Between 494 and 756 during the Pei Wei dynasty,
nearly two thousand caves were dug and 100,000 statues sculpted.

THE BLUE RIVER AND THE RED BASIN

Pursuing his course in the Wei valley, Marco crossed the Tsingling Mountains and descended into the plain of the Blue River, the Changjiang or Yang-tze, or as he called it, the Kiang-sui. He entered Manzi, a term used to designate what was left of the southern Sung empire. All that remained of this remarkable empire that had in the past encompassed most of China were a small part of the Yang-tze basin and a few southern provinces. When Marco Polo arrived, Kubilai Khan's troops were concluding their conquest. The last fortified towns were falling one after the other. As soon as he reached Manzi, Marco headed for the city of Ak-balik Manzi (present-day Hanzhong), located in the heart of a wooded area, where "lions and bears, lynx, hart, roebuck and stags , and so many of the beasts that produce musk" abounded. The region he described corresponded to the Han valley. Although it is mountainous, this area has since been stripped of most of its forests. The inhabitants burned them down to gain new arable land. The abundant wild life he mentioned has practically disappeared, despite the introduction of new species. Pesticides, industrial and natural pollution, plus the lack of environmental awareness of both the authorities and the farmers have contributed to this dramatic reversal.

The Blue River's other name in Chinese is "The Son of the Ocean." It is 5,980 kilometers long, the longest river in China. It rises in the Tibetan high plateaus and has a drainage basin of 1,800,000 square kilometers. In fact the name we know it by, the Yang-tze, really only refers to its lower course. Its real name is Changjiang or "Long River" and for a distance of 1,200 kilometers its middle section serves as the natural border between the two largest south-western provinces, Yunnan and Sichuan. Its upper course also forms the border between Sichuan and Tibet. It is only navigable downstream from Yibin after receiving the waters of its tributary, the Min, in the middle of the Red basin in Sichuan.

"When we went towards the west, twenty days' journey among the mountains, we found a plain and a province which [...] is called Sindufu. The main city [...] is also called Sindufu." This is how Marco Polo introduced the province cf Sichuan and its capital Chengdu, inhabited mainly, at that time, by Tibetans. The Hans systematically colonized these lands and little by little the Tibetans were forced to withdraw into the mountainous regions to the west where living conditions were more difficult, leaving the east, known as the Red Basin, to the new settlers. Considered the most densely populated agricultural area in the world, eastern Sichuan includes the Chengdu plain and an impressive series of low hills studded with cultivated terraces. The Red basin is one of the most fertile regions in southern China, if not the richest. Its complex irrigation system is several thousand years old. Even in Marco Polo's days farming was already remarkable and highly developed thanks to an ingenious system of dikes. Today it is known as the "granary of China." The mild climate makes it possible to bring in three harvests a year. Over the centuries, farmers have developed surprising successions of terraced fields for raising crops. Rice, wheat, corn, potatoes, vegetables, citrus fruits, sugar cane, peanuts, rape, sesame, tobacco and tea are only some of the local agricultural products. Chengdu (Sindufu in *Description of the World*) is over twenty-five centuries old and was described by Marco Polo as "a very great and noble city [...] (with) great and rich kings [...] and a multitude of ships." Today it is a large provincial metropolis and has only been opened to foreigners since 1978.

The development of a network of railways and roads since 1950 has favored its emergence as an agricultural center, whereas all the luster of its prestigious past has disappeared.

The source of the Blue River is on Mount Tanggula (or Keke Shili) in Qinghai. Unlike the Yellow River, it has many tributaries, particularly in the Red basin which has become the prime agricultural region of China.

*The Chengdu plain has the densest farming population in the world
and is the richest region of the Red basin.*

The plain benefits from the combined favors of an exceptionally clement climate
and extremely fertile alluvial deposits that in some places reach seventy meters.

Marco Polo's 'Tebet' included Tibet itself, part of southern Qinghai and western Sichuan,
where Tibetains are still the majority ethnic group.

The Province of Tebet and Kara-Jong

FROM WESTERN SICHUAN TO EASTERN TIBET AND YUNNAN

*Most of the inhabitants lead a semi-nomadic life.
When the good weather returns,
they set out in search of new pastures for their herds.*

*Certain commentators wonder
if Marco Polo really visited Tibet in person, or if he limited himself to gathering the information he had been told
concerning the province. As research stands at present, it appears that young Polo did go from Sichuan to eastern Tibet,
specifically the area contiguous to mountainous western Sichuan.*

MARCO POLO'S TEBET

Marco Polo's mention of Mongu Khan (Mongka Khan) seems to confirm this thesis. Indeed, Mongu, one of Kubilai's brothers, had been the Mongol's previous Great Khan. In 1258 he had sent his armies to subdue western Sichuan and the region near the Tibetan plateau. After a series of lightning victories, the Tartar soldiers had stopped, not advancing further into Tibetan territory. Thus, at the time of Marco Polo's travels, most of Tibet remained independent.

Tibetan peasants leaving a small monastery in Jinzhaigou.

Western Sichuan has remained one of China's most desolate regions. Incomes from livestock raising and farming are low and the inhabitants live in crowded poverty-stricken villages.

Sichuan is divided into two very different geographic entities. To the east lies the rich Red basin; to the west, the compact mass of the rugged eastern Himalayan foothills. When Marco Polo crossed these mountains, the population was Tibetan. To his mind, the area of present-day Sichuan was indisputably part of Tibet. Although many Chinese colonists of Han origin have settled in the region over the course of the centuries, and particularly starting with the 1911 Revolution, Tibetans are still the second ethnic group after the Hans. They earn a meager living from semi-itinerant farming and livestock raising on the wooded mountain slopes.

Western Sichuan, like neighboring Tibet, is extremely isolated from the rest of the country. Unlike the Red basin, this region has never benefited from road and rail projects linking it to other parts of the country. A blatant lack of economic and medical infrastructures only add to these communication difficulties. The unwieldy and petty Chinese administration weighs heavily on the everyday life of the people. The army is omnipresent, proof that Beijing is suspicious of the secessionist leanings in a region where Tibetan influence is widespread. The harsh climate and the difficulty of farming infertile soil on steep-sloped mountains contribute to making life even harder today than it was in the ancient Tebet of Marco Polo.

In the past, thousands of monks lived in monasteries.
The Cultural Revolution destroyed the latter and massacred or deported the former.
Yet, in the past few years, the Beijing regime has become slightly more tolerant as a result of international pressure;
now novices are returning to lamist schools.

Evening prayer in a monastery takes place to the sound of sacred horns and bells.

*Nestled against a mountain,
the Lhabrang (or Lapulengsi) lamasery in southern Qinghai
is the most important religious center of the gelupa
(Yellow Hats) outside of Tibet.
Four hundred monks live here, isolated among the Hui,
a Muslim people.*

Daily chores are allotted to the monks according to seniority and rank.
While masters study and meditate, helpers
and novices prepare the food and maintain the buildings.

A silver head ornament, enhanced
with semi-precious stones typical of the region.
In the Tibetan zone, the women of each ethnic group
wear their group's own headdress.

*Very few true **changpa**, nomads, still exist outside of Tibetan territory.*
They can only be seen on the high arid plateaus of western Sichuan.

The "black tents" these nomads live in got their name from the yak hair from which they are made.

STRANGE CUSTOMS

In these Tibetan provinces our intrepid thirteenth century traveler came across "deserted places where a host of wild animals roam." During stop-overs in the rare hamlets, he met idolaters who "live on hunting [...] and who give (to passing strangers) their daughters to do with as they wish and sleep with them [...]. And when these men have satisfied their every whim and are ready to set out again, it is the custom to give a little something, a jewel, a ring, a medal [...] to the girls [...] for, thus, when the time comes for them to marry, they will be able to furnish the proof that they had been loved and had had lovers [...]. These girls are held in high esteem and are more readily married off." This form of hospitality appeared and still appears scandalous to Western eyes. The Tibetans were foremost among the many Asian peoples to offer their daughters to travelers. This custom increased the value of the women in question because men from the outside world had found them to their liking. On the other hand, once married, they were expected to be irreproachably faithful. These traditions have changed, of course, owing to Chinese and Christian influences. Other customs, however, which at first glance may seem surprising, still survive in the Tibetan area. In fact, they were developed in response to necessity often related to the demands of a harsh environment. Polyandry, for instance, which allows a woman to marry several brothers, is simply a form of birth control, that is, a means of husbanding the meager resources of their poor soil.

*This woman selling knickknacks in a makeshift stall
illustrates the Tibetan tragedy.
What can an impoverished population do
against the all-powerful Chinese government?*

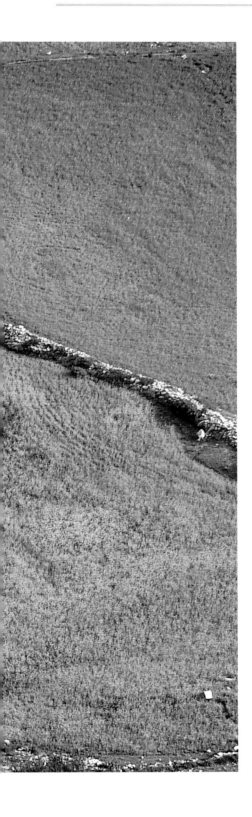

Tibetan women are known to be expert fabric dyers and weavers.
Many work in state owned workshops
that the provincial governments provide for them.

◁

Many Tibetans have settled in small villages and earn a meager living from mountain farming.
They sometimes raise cattle which they drive to summer pastures in May
and bring down again in September.

Agriculture has become increasingly important since the end of the last century.
Cereal farming is best adapted to the aridity of the land and the harsh climatic conditions.

YUNNAN

After Sichuan and eastern Tibet, Marco Polo continued his way towards Yunnan. It is most likely that he discovered it while accompanying the first Mongol expedition Kubilai's Muslim Uzbek friend, Nasr ed Din, led against Burma in 1277. After crossing the Yang-tze, Marco entered Yunnan from the north, into the province of Kara-jong, that is "the black kingdom." It was a non-Chinese state which Kubilai had conquered in 1253. He visited its capital, Yachi (present-day Kunming), renowned for its white porcelain. He then headed westward and saw the vast wooded mountainous region between the Salween and the Mekong valleys. It was known as Zar-dandan in Persian, that is "Golden Teeth" and got its name from the people's habit of covering their teeth with gold. The capital was Vochan, probably present-day Baoshan. On several occasions Marco Polo indicated some of the specific local customs. Although man-childbed or what ethnologists call couvade has disappeared today, except in

some remote valleys in Xishuangbanna, it was the strangest custom Marco Polo came across. After the birth of a child, the mother returns directly to work, while the father "goes to bed and takes the baby with him, and stays in bed for forty days, without leaving it [...] (for he) must also have his share of trouble."

Yunnan is also the hub of the Tibetan, Burman and southern Chinese area. A multitude of ethnic groups have lived side by side here for nearly one thousand years. The Yi (or Lolo), the Bai (or Pai), the Dai (or Thai), the Hani (or Woni), the Lisu, the Lahu, the Wa and the Naxi are some of the twenty-three ethnic groups that have been counted in Yunnan today. Their festivities, their brightly colored clothing and their gold, mother-of-pearl and amber headdresses are all a delight to the foreign visitor. Their languages, cultures and tribal organization constitute a treasure for linguists and ethnologists.

A little Miao-tze girl.
Her people are famous for their passion for dancing.

*A Bai village. The Bai (or Pai), also known as Ber Dser or Per Tsu,
are considered to be the original population of the ancient kingdom of Nanchao.*

A Lahu woman grinding hard wheat in a traditional mortar.

*The brightly colored, expertly designed women's costumes
of the minority ethnic groups in Yunnan are remarkable.
Here, some Lisu and a Lahu woman and her baby.
In these tribal societies the women are guardians of tradition.*

As one goes south, the environment becomes more tropical.
One encounters the Palaung and the Va (or Wa) tribes.

Isolated in their mountains in the southernmost parts of Yunnan
(which Marco Polo probably did not visit) numerous ethnic groups live peaceably,
far from main thoroughfares and political events.

▷

The surprising diversity of cultures and ethnic groups which has been Burma's trademark
has also made it a difficult country to govern.

A typical street scene in northeastern Burma.

The Kingdom of Mien

AN EXPEDITION TO BURMA

In 1277 Kubilai Khan's troops invaded the high valleys of Burma and swept down on the kingdom of Mien (present-day Pagan), whose sovereign also reigned over the kingdom of Bengala, which corresponds to the eastern part of Bengal. In 1285 the Great Khan ordered a new Mongol invasion. Finally, in 1287-1288 a third expedition penetrated deep into Burma, subduing it definitively and condemning it to pay heavy tribute to the Tartars.

A STRANGE RICH COUNTRY

Description of the World informs us that after a "long descent" following the Irrawaddy valley, one reaches "a great province, lying toward the south, on the confines of India, the name of which is Mien." The questions raised about some of Marco Polo's destinations are again appropriate here. Did the Venetian visit the kingdom of Mien as he claims? If so, when and in what conditions? Once again, there is no easy answer. Certain parts of his account have obviously been borrowed, but what he reports about northern Burma seems to be based on personal observation, probably made during the first Mongol expedition against the kingdom of Mien, and perhaps also after 1287, when the capital fell to Kubilai's armies.

The middle course of the Salween, in Burma, has remained untouched by modern civilization.
Activities such as the market or a train of tropical hardwood floating on the water,
all take place at the traditional slow rhythm.

WILD ANIMALS AND NATURAL WEALTH

Marco Polo was impressed by the rich vegetation covering the northern and central regions of the province of Mien. "It takes a fortnight to cross," he writes in *Description of the World*, through very inaccessible places and through vast jungles teeming with elephants, unicorns and other wild beasts."

The forest Marco Polo speaks of exists and covers nearly all of the northern region. It contains some rare varieties of trees, such as teak, which has been exploited since the seventeenth

The tiger, the symbol of Burma, is now practically extinct.

Lake Inle, at an altitude of 1,000 meters, is dotted with floating islands on which the Intha have built tiny hamlets.

century. In the central region, however, the forest has been destroyed by slash-and-burn farming practices and has practically disappeared. Despite efforts by the Burmese government to teach villagers the dangers of destroying their vital natural environment, destruction continues. The disappearance of many of the animal species Marco Polo saw is the most visible consequence. There are hardly any large mammals left. The intensive hunts led by the British during the colonial period eliminated the tigers and rhinoceroses. The elephants have managed to survive only because they were domesticated for work in the fields and forests.

In the past, the kingdom of Mien had sizable gold mines and precious stone mines. Blood will tell ! As the worthy son of Niccolo, Marco tried to trade in the latter. He noticed with great interest that the local inhabitants possessed large quantities of gold, but were not allowed to take it out of the country. They could only exchange it for money from merchants coming from India and China. *Description of the World* offers us no details as to the amount of profit the young Venetian made during his stay.

Burma was long considered the Asian El Dorado because of its mineral wealth. Although outdated techniques and equipment are still being used, the mines continue to furnish precious stones and gold. Profits, however, are plummeting, as the quality of the products has been judged insufficient on the world market. In the thirties petroleum was discovered and despite the country's technological backwardness, this new resource has been yielding considerable income.

The Irrawaddy, navigable for two-thirds of its 2,100 kilometers, is the longest river in the country.
It is also the principal means of communication and trade between the various provinces,
which accounts for the incessant activity along its banks.

In Mandalay, the colorful sight of buffaloes transporting teak towards a river early in the morning.

*The inhabitants of the Mont Popa region
gather succulent palm honey
that is then mixed with fresh yogurt.*

Burma is the land of pagodas.
A seventeenth century saying claims that there were at least two per inhabitant!

THE COUNTRY OF PAGODAS

The city of Mien mentioned by Marco Polo corresponds to the present city of Pagan. The Burmans had made it their capital in 849 A.D. In the eleventh century they became the masters of Burma which had theretofore been dominated by the Mons whose capital was Thaton. The introduction of Theravada Buddhism in Burma allowed the reigning dynasties to establish close cultural, political and military ties with other Buddhist countries, like Sri Lanka. Innumerable sumptuous pagodas and monasteries were then built throughout the kingdom of Pagan. The current grandeur of the monuments that have survived Burma's troubled history are in no way inferior to what the thirteenth century traveler already saw. "The king [...] ordered [...] that two round towers be

*A procession of effigies of Buddha
during Thingyan in Taunggyi.*

At the top of Mount Popa, at an altitude of 1,520 meters, is a little white-walled,
gold-roofed sanctuary dedicated to Mahagiri nat (protective spirits).
It is one of the holiest places in the Pagan area.

erected, one of gold and one of silver, such as I shall describe: for one tower was built of fine stones and then covered with a finger's thickness of gold. It was so completely covered that it appeared to be made only of gold [...]. The other tower was of silver and quite similar."

Today the city of Pagan, as well as the whole province of Mandalay in which it is located, is one of the marvels that history has bequeathed to mankind. Some five thousand pagodas are spread across 23 square kilometers. According to tradition, it was called "the city of four million pagodas," and more than thirteen thousand are said to have been counted at the height of its glory. The recognizable red-brick Hindu sanctuaries blend harmoniously with the white-washed Buddhist edifices. The interiors are decorated with immense statues and superb bas-reliefs. Watching the sun set on this magnificent site as the last rays tint the golden cupolas red is an unforgettable sight.

The style of Burmese statues combines Chinese fondness
for rotundity and southeast Asian finesse.

At the end of the eighteeenth century King Bodawpaya invested his visions of grandeur in the city of Mingun.
He wanted to erect the biggest Buddhist monuments ever built.
The gigantic pagoda Mantara Gyi and an enormous bell,
weighing eighty-seven tons and measuring eight meters in height, were constructed here.
The pagoda was destroyed by an earthquake in 1838 and is now the largest heap of bricks in the world.

Buddhism plays an important role in society.
Every male is expected to make a stay in a monastery while a teen-ager.

An enchanting sunset over Pagan,
seen from the terrace of Thatbyinnyu.

*Gigantic statues of Buddha in his multiple incarnations
can be found inside Buddhist pagodas.*

General view of Pagan, nicknamed "the city of four thousand pagodas."
There once were over five thousand, of which 2,300 are extant today.
Pagan was the capital of Burma from 1044 to 1287.
The palaces and houses were built of wood, the pagodas, of brick or stone.
When Kubilai Khan's troops captured the city, everything was burnt down,
except the magnificent sanctuaries

▷

The famous fishermen on stilts from Weligama
and the beautiful women of Trincomalee have had their reputation made long ago.

Fishermen mending their nets on the beach at Udappuwa.

The Island of Seilan
A MISSION TO SRI LANKA

The substratum of Sri Lanka
is believed to be one of the richest in the world for sapphires, topazes, garnets, amethysts and especially rubies.
Even if their quality is not always up to scratch, the reputation of these Singhalese stones is firmly established.

THE BIGGEST RUBY IN THE WORLD

In 1284 Kubilai Khan sent his ambassador Marco Polo to the court of Parakramabahu III, king of Sri Lanka or the island of Seilan. According to a legend, this king owned, among other riches, a ruby "a palm in length, and of the thickness of a man's arm [...] and glowing red like fire." Despite the obvious exaggeration, this gem seems to have existed. In *Description of the World* we learn that Marco was one of the Tartar ambassadors. He did, indeed, see the famous gem and was very surprised : "I saw that ruby with my own eyes; when the lord held it in his closed hand, it protruded both above and below his fist."

Collective fishing is an ancient practice among the Singhalese.
Modern techniques and the profit motive, however, are hastening its disappearance.

The precise aim of Marco's mission remains vague. Very likely, as the Great Khan's envoy, he was to try to buy the famous ruby, whatever the price, also, to negotiate trade agreements for the purchase of precious gems, as well as to obtain from the Singhalese ruler an act of allegiance to the Mongol crown. He was not able to procure the glorious gem, but he did return with a treaty of alliance making Parakramabahu a vassal of the Tartar throne.

At the time, the Singhalese were already Buddhists and not warlike. Marco learned that if they were in need of weapons, they had to import them. Alas, the situation has changed radically since that time. In 1983 a dreadful civil war broke about between the Hindu Tamil population from the north and the rest of the country which is Buddhist. Since then, guerrilla operations and government reprisals have followed, with the unfortunate Singhalese people caught in the middle as hostages; tens of thousands have been killed.

The design of the *oruva*,
these high narrow Singhalese boats
from Negombo is quite typical.
The *karava*, local fisherman, equip them
with out-riggers and a reddish sail.

The countryside at Nuwara Eliya.
This region, located at an altitude of 1,900 meters,
was a summer resort first for Singhalese rulers,
then in the nineteenth century for English officers
and today for modern tourists

Despite its altitude of 2,000 meters, the Ella region has numerous rice fields and is said to produce the best quality rice.

"Ceylan tea," which made Sri Lanka famous nearly two hundred years ago, was, in fact, imported by the British, as was coffee and hevea.

The Ruvanvelisaya stupa in Anuradhapura and the Gal Vihara in Polonnaruw.
These two dead cities were the early capitals of the kings of Sri Lanka during, the thirteenth and third centuries respectively.
Anuradhapura and the city of Mihintale were also the birthplaces of Singhalese Buddhism.

The most famous monument in Kandy is the Dalada Maligawa or Temple of the Tooth.
It houses one of Buddha's teeth which, according to tradition, was saved from his funeral pyre.
It is believed to have been brought to Sri Lanka around 301
and to have finally arrived in Kandy after numerous adventures.

BUDDHA'S TEETH

The Great Khan's messengers returned without the prestigious ruby. Instead, in addition to the treaty of alliance, they brought sacred relics : two teeth, a lock of hair and a green porphyry vessel ! According to an ancient tradition, the remains of Sagamoni Burcan, that is Cakyamuni, the historical Buddha, could be found on the mountain of Adam, known by Buddhists as Samanala or Sri Pada. The Saracens claimed that the biblical Adam and this Buddha, the first man to be worshiped as a god, were one and the same person. The relics Marco Polo gave to Kubilai were supposed to have been from this holy place. The Mongol monarch was delighted with the gift. Rumor had it that if food for one man were placed in the porphyry vessel, it would multiply to feed at least five !

The sanctuary itself is in Kandy, a picturesque little town in the center of Sri Lanka, nestled in steep mountains along the Mahaweli Ganga River, the longest in the country. The most famous monument is the Temple of the Tooth, which got its name from one of Buddha's teeth which has been preserved in a reliquary consisting of six golden caskets fitting one into the other. Saved from Buddha's funeral pyre in northern India, it miraculously got to Anuradhapura in 313 A.D. hidden in a princess's headdress.

Throughout the year thousands of pilgrims and the faithful come from all over the world to give homage to the prestigious relic.

Village scenes near Ba Na and Mi Son.

◁

*Rice growing in flooded paddies
is the most common farming technique used in Vietnam.
It is believed to have been invented in the lower Yang-tze basin
towards the ninth century, later spreading over all southeast Asia.*

When Marco entered the kingdom of Tonking and Annam he was struck by the rugged mountains of northern Vietnam, as well as by the dense forests that cover them even today. Over the course of history this inhospitable region has often served as a refuge for Indochinese guerrillas. As we know, neither the Sungs nor Mao Zedong, not to mention the Mongols, the French or the Americans, were able to subdue these fierce fighters who instinctively knew

A pepper plant plantation on the western high plateaus. A peasant woman returning from the fields after a hard day's work.

how to live in symbiosis with their environment. Marco was less impressed by the political power of the king than by the appearance of many of the ethnic groups which composed his kingdom. The only remark he felt he ought to tell us about Indravarman was, "this lecherous king [...] has over three hundred wives." The inhabitants of the two provinces he visited, Kaugigu and Amu, surprised him by their appearance; the bodies of both the men and the women of the kingdom of Tonking were decorated with tattoos. Marco Polo marveled at the art of the master tattooers who "using a needle, covered all the flesh with pictures of lions and dragons and eagles and cranes [...] they are made so skillfully with needles that they are indelible, whether in water or otherwise. They make these on their faces, their necks, their bellies, their hands, their legs and every part of their bodies." This practice was first forbidden by the French colonial administration, then by the Communists, but reappeared in the 1960's. Today, the ethnic groups of the high plateaus such as the Bana, the Jarai and the M'nongs proudly display their traditional tattoos. In the province of Amu, the people Marco met were not tattooed; instead they wore heavy gold and silver bracelets enhanced with precious stones and pearls both on their arms and legs. There too, despite the vicissitudes of history, the old customs have returned. Increasingly often the women, in particular, make and wear splendid headdresses and jewels respecting the ancient tradition.

The complex of religious buildings in Po Inu Nagar, "The Mistress of the Kingdom," includes several temples of striking architectural beauty with altars dedicated to Shiva. The best preserved buildings date from the eighth and ninth centuries.

There are innumerable ethnic groups on the southern high plateaus, all of whom, (the M'nong, the Jarai and the Bana, etc.) jealously defend their ancient traditions from the influences of the lowland Vietnamese whom they strongly distrust.

A young girl from Jining in Shandong.

One of the superb statues sheltered by the famous cliffs
of the Thousand Buddhas in Qixia Shan.
In the seventh century Liang emperor Wu
had some four hundred niches dug for the five hundred
statues of the Buddhist pantheon.

Modern China has inherited many gardens and navigable portions of the historic Grand Canal.
Here, in Suzhou and Wuxi.

The Province of Manzi
FROM SHANDONG TO FUJIAN

A s we have already seen,
the province of Manzi that Marco Polo visited consisted only of the western Changjiang basin and the present-day
provinces of Zhejiang, Jiangxi and Fujian. These are but a minute part of the prestigious empire of the southern Sungs.
The rulers of this dynasty had created south of the Huanghe an immense empire protected both by the strength
of their armies and the subtlety of their elaborate diplomacy.

THE MARVELOUS EMPIRE OF THE SOUTHERN SUNGS

Under their reign, southern China experienced the finest artistic and cultural development in its history ; this was the period specialists have recognized as the apogee of Chinese classicism. The empire, however, was unable to resist the repeated attacks of its northern rivals, first the Khitans, then the Juchen and their successors the Jins and finally the Yuans who achieved their final conquest at the time of the Polos stay in China. It was, therefore, the remains of an empire on its last legs, still struggling against the Mongol power, that Marco Polo visited several times, on private or official missions.

211

The lower course of the Blue River and its tributaries water an area with many large cities
(Nanjing, Suzhou, Yangshou, etc), as well as the metropolis of Shangaï.
It is not uncommon to come across traditional scenes within this modern universe.
Here, in a snake restaurant old peasants from Jiangsu are busy bargaining.

The Grand Canal is one of the principal achievements of Sung power. It was dug thanks to the determination of the Emperor Yangdi of the Suis who had the existing sections linked together. Starting at the end of the sixth century, Chinese rulers had tried to improve the irrigation and communication systems between the regions of Peking and the Huanghe and Yang-tze basins. The Grand Canal was opened between 587 and 608 A.D. and was later extended to Rongyang at the beginning of the fifteenth century. Complete with tiered locks, inclines for loading and unloading merchandise from the banks, and tunnels hollowed out of the mountains, this extraordinary engineering accomplishment remained the main waterway for Chinese trade until the nineteenth century, although the amount of traffic had been declining since the fifteenth century. Agricultural products traveled northward and manufactured products southward along the 1,800 kilometers linking Peking and Hangzhou.

It traversed four provinces, and opened communication among the five biggest waterways of eastern China. *Description of the World* unites in one memorable voyage along the Grand Canal several trips Marco took in Manzi, guiding us through the "rich and beautiful cities" of Changlu, Changli, Tandinfu, Sinju Matu, Linju, Pinju, Siju, Hwai-ngan-chau, Pao-ying, Kaoyu, Tai-chau, Chinju, Yang-chau, Ngan-king, Sinju, Kwa-chau, Chin-kiang-fu, Chang-chau, Su-chau, Vuju, Vughin, Changan and Kinsai which correspond to the present-day towns of Cangzhou, Dezhou, Dongping, Jining, Xuzhou, Peixian, Suquian, Huaian, Boaying, Gaoyou, Taizhou, Haian, Yangzhou, Nankin, Yizheng, Guazhou, Zhenjiang, Chanzhou, Suzhou, Wujiang, Jiaxing, Ciangan and Hangzhou.

OLD SALT TOWNS AND THE CITY OF HANGZHOU

The reasons for Kubilai Khan's sending Marco Polo to Manzi were more of an economic than a political nature, and foremost among them was the need to control and direct salt production. Indeed, many of the main cities in Manzi owed their wealth and importance to the fact that for centuries they had been centers of rock salt extraction and trading. Thus Changlu, Chinju and Sinju (present-day Cangzhou, Haian, Yizheng) were described by Marco as towns "where very great quantities of salt are produced everywhere."

According to his report the inhabitants "derive great profit and the Great Lord a handsome income." River trade was extremely dense; he wrote, "I can tell you that one day when I was in the town of Sinju, I counted at one time over fifteen thousand ships."

Unfortunately, very little of what Marco Polo saw can still be seen today. The remaining sections of the Grand Canal are few and far between. Most of the old sections have been diverted, abandoned or even covered with buildings. River traffic on this great thoroughfare has completely stopped. The temples and historical monuments on its banks were destroyed by the Manchus in the seventeenth century and then by Mao's iconoclastic soldiers. Several very beautiful gardens that once belonged to merchant-patrons during the Sung era still exist, particularly in Suzhou and Yangzhou, as do a few venerable pagodas in Jining, Yangzhou and Zhenjiang. Less attractive for the tourist are the highly polluted industrial and agricultural zones. This, however, is not true of Hangzhou. As we know, Marco Polo was the governor from 1282 to 1285. He was commissioned by Kubilai Khan to "see and hear the account of the Great Lord's annual income." The figures quoted in *Description of the World* and confirmed by the imperial registers offer a good idea of the economic importance of both the region and its governor which yielded the Mongol crown twenty-six tons of gold from the salt trade and fifty-eight more from various industries and businesses.

Marco Polo was particularly sensitive to the charm of this city which held a strategic position on the Grand Canal and whose canals and flat-bottomed boats reminded him of his native Venice. Today Hangzhou has the reputation of being the Chinese's favorite city. According to a famous saying "if the earthly paradise exists, one city on earth challenges its primacy, Hangzhou." The modern city is only thirty years old and of no interest. The surrounding countryside, however, with its tiny gardens and carefully farmed fields, its picturesque little houses amidst delicate gardens, as well as several beautiful pagodas, attract urban dwellers tired of the impersonal metropolis.

1291 - 1295
The Return Voyage

Cambalu, in the year 1291. It was now twenty years since the Polos had left home,
and almost eighteen that they had stayed in China. **Description of the World** tells us that, although the Polos "were very
rich in expensive jewels and in gold, they cherished an ardent desire to see their own land again.
And although they were honored and among the Khan's favorites, they dreamt of nothing else."
According to Marco Polo's accounts, the Great Khan had until then obstinately refused to let them leave. Kubilai Khan
was over seventy-five years old. The crown prince was dead and the court nobles and lamas were taking more
and more liberties as the monarch grew weaker. The Khan no doubt depended heavily on his three Venetian friends
in whom he had great confidence. An event, however, was to force him to let the Polos go. Arghun, the Khan of Persia,
lost his wife Bulagan (Bulughan) who was a Baya'ut, a tribe known for the beauty of its women. He wanted at all costs
to replace his deceased wife with a woman from the same tribe, so Kubilai Khan chose for him a young seventeen-year-old
Baya'ut, called Kokachin (Koikoitchin). She was delivered to emissaries the Khan of the Levant had sent,
but after six months of the return journey, fighting among the Mongol clans of central Asia brought their expedition
to a halt. The Golden Horde led by Kaidu allowed no one to travel towards Persia. The expedition, therefore, had to
return to Cambalu. As the land route was cut off, someone had to be found who could bring the princess to Arghun by sea.
All this took place just as the Polos were returning from a mission in India.
Having heard that the Venetians desired to see their homeland again, the Khan of the Levant's emissaries
"sought out the Great Khan and asked him to send them by sea with the three Latins, knowing that the foreigners
had seen and recognized most of the Indian Sea and the countries they had to traverse."
Overcoming his reluctance, Kubilai Khan finally accepted to let Marco, Niccolo and Maffeo go.

Lesser Java

FROM THE CHINESE COAST TO NORTHERN SUMATRA

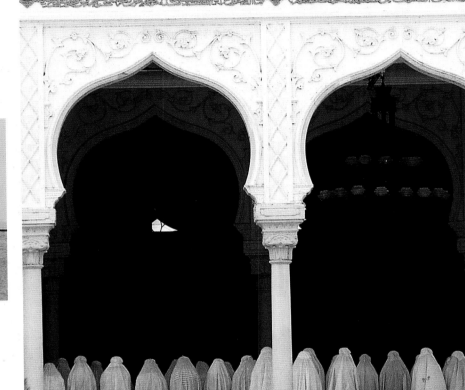

Travelers heading for Sumatra encounter the Muslim world at the Con Dao archipelago (Marco Polo knew them as the islands of Sundor and Condur).

The small group fetched into the port of Zaiton, present-day Qangzhou in Fujian. It is quite likely that Marco Polo had already embarked several times from here for India. He would then proceed to navigate along the Vietnamese shoreline before reaching the Indian coast, thus, in fact, preparing his final voyage home.

THE BEGINNING OF A PEACEFUL VOYAGE

Description of the World does not furnish enough information to know where, when and how many times the young Venetian visited what he calls Greater India. The only facts we are given concern the Polos' last voyage to this faraway country. "Then, Messer Marco was returning from a certain mission in India for his Lordship; he had followed various maritime routes and had on many occasions brought back news of this land [...]. Messer Polo had stayed in India for so long, and made so many return trips, and researched and questioned so much that either by hearsay or by sight he knew and had seen everything." One could not be clearer. Our inveterate traveler, accompanied by his father, Niccolo, and his uncle, Maffeo, were indeed returning from an official mission.

The Malaysian and Indonesian populations of the Rian archipelago and the northwest coast of Sumatra earn their living principally from fishing.

This final voyage could only have taken place in 1290 or 1291, for immediately after it, the three Venetians set off for Europe.

So, in 1291 the three Venetians and princess Kokachin left Fujian, accompanied by three ambassadors of Khan Arghun and a large escort, consisting of a squadron of fourteen junks manned by six hundred sailors. They crossed the Gulf of Cheynam (the present-day Gulf of Tonkin) leaving the coast of Champa (present-day Vietnam) in the distance. They then doubled the islands of Sondur and Condur (the present-day islands of Con Son), then Pentan (present-day Bintan) located south of the Malaysian peninsula and touched land in the north of Lesser Java, or Sumatra, after three months of uneventful sailing.

They were to stay there for five months. In order to protect themselves against wild animals and the hostile local populations they constructed five fortified encampments.

ACEH COUNTRY

According to Marco Polo there were eight kingdoms on Sumatra and he visited six of them which he called Ferlec, Basman, Sumatra, Dagroian, Lambri and Fansur. These kingdoms correspond to the northwest part of the biggest Indonesian island. The inhabitants subsisted on the many natural riches of the land. "This island abounds in treasures and in costly spices, including aloe wood, spikenard, brazil, ebony and many other spices that never reach our country." The kingdoms of Ferlec and Lambri correspond approximately to today's Aceh province. Cannibalistic Muslims lived there, said Marco Polo ! For him to have so emphasized the religious aggressiveness of the natives reveals how uncomfortable he must have felt confronted with the strong Muslim extremism in Aceh country. Things have not changed much since then, excepting the cannibalism which was already rare in the thirteenth century and has long since disappeared. Aceh country is still home to the strongest form of Muslim fundamentalism in Indonesia. The population is of two sorts : the ethnic groups from the mountainous interior, such as the Gajos and the Ala peoples, and the coastal tribes. The former are general taller than the average Indonesian and are known to practice a particularly strict, even xenophobic, form of Islam. Over the centuries their ancestors fought off all the powers which tried to conquer them. One of the bloodiest rebellions of southeast Asia took place here between 1873 and 1877, when all the tribes of the Aceh region rose up against the

Built entirely of wood and assembled without a single nail, the superb Raya mosque is the most holy sanctuary of Banda Aceh. It was raised by the Dutch at the beginning of the twentieth century as a sign of good will on the ruins of the mosque that had been burnt down when Sumatra was invaded from the north.

The graceful design of the long fishing sailboats is perfect for navigating in the open sea where sudden violent storms are common.

Dutch occupation. The Europeans lost over two hundred and fifty thousand men and two generals during the conflict. Walking around the streets of the provincial capital, Banda Aceh, the modern visitor is more likely to imagine he is in Saudi Arabia than in Indonesia. It is, for example, the only place in Asia where foreigners must imperatively fast during Ramadan. Numerous restrictions concerning clothing and behavior in public are imposed, especially on women. A lack of respect for these rules is taken as an offense. The imprudent foreigner who persists in his ways runs the risk of suffering what may be "painful" consequences.

*The island's last orang-outangs
live in a nature reserve forest
in the northwest point of Sumatra.*

RARE ANIMALS

The kingdom of Basman that Marco Polo described corresponded to the former kingdom of Pasai, which latter became Sumatra. Here the Venetians encountered some surprising wild animals, "elephants, unicorns and others." Marco wrote of the one-horned rhinoceros, which is today an endangered species: "they are very ugly and disgusting brutes to look at," and, contrary to rumor, "they do not let themselves be captured by the breast." He also countered the popular idea that they were so tame they could be captured by maidens. This text is interesting, first of all, because it illustrates that Marco's curiosity was aroused by everything he saw, not only by human society. Then, it proves, if need be, the constant concern for truth that permeates his account.

In the forests of northern Sumatra there were still other creatures that intrigued the three Venetians. "On this island there is a sort of monkey which is very tiny and has a face very like a man's." According to Marco, men captured these monkeys, boiled them and removed their hair, except the beard. Then they were treated with saffron and camphor and their skin was painted "so that it looked like human skin." Finally, they were dried and "arranged [...] so that they appeared to be human." These false men were no other than ourang-outangs, which literally means "men of the forest" in Indonesian. The large, anthropomorphic apes, with their long arms and sparse red hair, were often taken for wild men much like our early prehistoric

Today, the northwest is completely agricultural.
The forests have been cut down by generations of poor farmers
in an effort to increase the amount of arable land.

ancestors. From the eighteenth century on scientists have been studying these pongidae, mankind's cousins. Fewer than two hundred of them are still extant in a national nature reserve in the forests of northern Sumatra, not far from Bukit Lawang, undoubtedly the region Marco Polo visited. Indeed, every day at set times, the apes come for the food forest rangers put out for them on tree platforms.

Batak country

Although the genesis of the name Dagroian is unknown, it must have designated the Lake Toba region, the mythical place from which all the Batak clans originated. It covers 800 square kilometers and is 80 kilometers long, resembling a small inland sea rather than a lake. It is, indeed, the biggest lake in Asia and one of the deepest (around 500 meters) as well as one of the highest in the world (over 900 meters). It is surrounded by magnificent pine-covered mountains. Its usually calm blue waters occasionally turn dark black at the outbreak of one of the violent storms for which it is famous. The lake is in the center of a region inhabited exclusively by Batak peoples. According to a legend Marco Polo recounts, the Bataks, whom the Venetian knew to be idolaters, that is, Buddhists, were "from the same island." He is referring to the small island of Samosir, located in the middle of the lake.

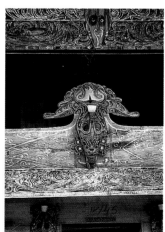

The Batak are the only inhabitants of Sumatra that earn their living exclusively from farming;
most of the other ethnic groups depend upon the sea for their livelihood.
They have perpetuated certain traditions that date back to neolithic times,
when their ancestors settled in the mountains near Lake Toba. They are famous for their unusual roofs.

This is where the Batak peoples - the Tobas, the Karos (whose territory must have corresponded to the kingdom of Fensur mentioned in *Description of the World*), the Simalunggun and the Mandailing - originate. The former are Christians, the latter Muslims and the others still conserve certain animistic practices. Despite their cultural differences, they all have in common the traditional custom of constructing superb wooden homes with their characteristic roofs. Each ethnic group has its own type of roof and the size, shape and decoration indicate the clan, the seniority and the wealth of the family. Two other of Marco's observations are of particular interest to us. First and foremost, the importance within these communities of the priest-healers, about whom the young Venetian noted that they were "prophets or magicians [...] who said that they knew by means of their diabolic enchantments and their idols whether the patient is to recover or to die." The second is their use of the sago tree, a palm tree whose pith provides sago, a flour used to make flatbread. The description Marco gives is still applicable today : "These trees are full of flour [...] and so (the people) take the flour from these trees and put it in troughs full of water and stir it with a stick, so that the

*The production of sago from the sago palm tree no longer exists on Sumatra
although it can be seen on the small Mentawai archipelago to the southwest.*

husks and impurities float on the surface and are thrown away, whereas the pure flour settles to the bottom. This done, the water is poured off and the clean flour is left heaped at the bottom. It is then made into dough from which many excellent dishes are made." To observe this procedure today it is necessary to visit the Mentawi islands, a small archipelago to the southwest of Sumatra.

A fishing scene along the Coromandel coast.

Many elephants have been imported from India
to work in the forests of the Andaman and Nicobar archipelagoes.

▷

Fishing is the mainstay of villagers
along the southern coast of India.

The Province of Maabar
FROM THE NICOBAR ISLANDS TO THE COROMANDEL COAST

The Polo's fleet left Sumatra and headed north-west.
They soon came upon the Islands of Necuveran and Angaman, present-day Nicobar and Andaman,
which belong to India. We do not know if they actually landed on Nicobar or simply sailed past it.
In any case, Marco noted that "in this island (the inhabitants) have neither king nor lord
but are like wild beasts [...] they go stark naked."

THE NEGRITOS' ISLANDS

They could not have dropped anchor in Andaman, for he reported sailor's rumors to the effect that "all the men of this island have heads like dogs, and teeth and eyes like dogs." The inhabitants of Andaman were then supposed to be dog-headed! As they are the direct descendants of the Negritos, the oldest population stock in this part of the world, the ethnic groups that populate this archipelago constitute an exceptional testimony to the human species. Their principal characteristics are their small stature, dark skin, Negroid features and kinky hair. Despite the efforts of the Indian government to protect them, they are becoming extinct; there are fewer than two hundred members in even the largest groups. It is extremely difficult to obtain an authorization to approach them and even more

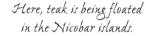

Negrito features are characteristic
of the primitive ethnic groups
of Andaman and Nicobar.

▷

Here, teak is being floated
in the Nicobar islands.

Buffaloes bathing in the Mannar Gulf
after a day's work in the fields.

difficult to meet authentic members of the Shompen tribe in Nicobar and Jarawa, or Sentinels and Onges in Andaman. The most traditional continue their primitive ways of life in the dense forests that cover the island highlands. The others who are of mixed Indian or Asian blood, subsist in the coastal areas thanks to the income they obtain from fishing and turtle hunting.

THE COROMANDEL COAST

The Polos continued their journey westward. They soon came in view of the Indian coastline. It is difficult to determine if they first stopped in Sri Lanka or if they headed straight for the Indian sub-continent and later made their excursion to Sri Lanka. The fact remains that they touched the shores of India, Greater India, as Marco called it, in the great province of Maabar, which is not to be mistaken for the present-day Malabar coast. The name Maabar was given to the Coromandel coast, the south-eastern part of the Indian peninsula, by tenth-century Arab navigators. Coromandel is the French form of the Indian, Chola Mandalam, that is, "Country of the Cholas," one of the oldest peoples and dynasties of southern India whose culture flourished from the first to the eleventh century. The state of Tamil Nadu today corresponds to ancient Chola Mandalam. One finds there a great number of imposing temples and palaces that testify not only to the glorious past of the Cholas, but also to that of the Pallavas and the Pandyas who contributed some of the finest monuments in the area. At the time the

Venetians' fleet arrived in southeastern India, the Coromandel ports were experiencing a period of economic prosperity. Most of the trade with China, Sri Lanka, Malaysia and Indonesia was shipped from these ports. Fishing and fish by-products were an additional source of income for the inhabitants. These two activities have been in constant decline since the seventeenth century and today the traditional fishing industry is insignificant. The villagers do not have the means to compete with the large, often foreign, ships that fish on an industrial scale off their coast. Their peaceful life has been disrupted by the creation of large industrial, business and agricultural centers around the major economic hubs such as Madras, which, with its five and a half million inhabitants, has become the fourth largest city in India.

A small street market in Bandar, formerly known as Masulipatnam.

GOLCONDE DIAMONDS

It is possible that Marco Polo may have visited these regions on earlier missions for Kubilai Khan, but his book makes no mention of it. In any event, the Venetian's fleet went up the Indian coast in a northern direction. In a small town which was probably present-day Mailapuram, he claims, mistakenly, to have visited the tomb of the apostle Saint Thomas. Following this, Marco Polo came to the kingdom of Motupalli, a thousand miles to the north. Motupallii was the name of the Hindu state of Telingana, located in the eastern part of today's Andhra Pradesh and the southern part of Orissa. Its name was derived from the Telugu languages spoken by the inhabitants. Shortly after Marco's visit the kingdom was conquered by the Sultan of Delhi and Hinduism was replaced by Islam, still the predominant religion in the region today. Marco recorded that the snake-infested Motupalli mountains concealed the largest diamond lodes of the continent. The *Book of Marvels* indicates the main techniques used at the time to extract the precious gems. One of them has clearly been exaggerated by legend: the inhabitants are said to throw pieces of meat into deep ravines so that the diamonds become embedded in the flesh. Eagles, which are abundant in the region, then

The Golconde fort was built by sultan Quli Qutub Shah in the sixteenth century.
One can still see armories, warehouses, grain silos and,
scattered around the old city, canons of various eras.

General view of the fortifications in old Golconde.
The opulent trading center which dominated
this part of Dekkan in Marco Polo's times,
was transformed into an impregnable stronghold
three centuries later by the Muslim Shahi dynasty.
It was surrounded by three high defensive walls,
the outermost of which was nearly six kilometers long.

come to eat the meat and take to the air. Later, the people either collect the diamonds from the eagles' droppings or by opening their bellies.

Surrounded by five kilometers of walls and defended by eighty-seven bastions, the fortified city of Golkonda (Golconde) was destroyed in 1687 by the Mogul emperor Aurangzeb. It has always been associated with diamonds, which have been the source of its wealth since the sixteenth century (it was founded in 1512) and it has been given the nickname of "the city of diamonds." The diamond mines in the surrounding area, however, had been worked for many years when Marco visited there and generated profitable business in the town on whose site

prestigious Golconde was to be built. One must not forget that the elder Polos were well-known gemmologists and must have shown a keen interest in this diamond industry. Marco had a marvelous memory of the region. He could not have suspected that centuries later the fabulous Koh-i-noor would be discovered there and that Golconde would become the biggest diamond market in the world.

In present-day Golconde there has been no diamond mining for a long time. It has become a sleepy average-sized town lost in the Dekkan heat, forgotten both by tourists and diamond professionals and yet impressive ruins of its past splendor remain.

GULF OF MANNAR PEARLS

Heading south, the Polos entered the Gulf of Mannar, between India and Sri Lanka. They followed it till they reached "the noble city of Cail," which corresponds to the small town of Palayakal, not far from Tirunelveli. At the time it was an important intermediate port for maritime trade. The region was renowned for both the quantity and quality of its pearls, and in the gulf they saw a multitude of pearl divers' boats. It was a seasonal occupation and from October to December, during the easterly monsoons, when navigation was dangerous, the pearl divers stayed ashore. But as soon as good weather returned, particularly in April and May, they set out again in search of pearl oysters, sometimes going as far as the Gulf of Bettala (now Puttalam in Sri Lanka). To protect themselves against the dangerous sharks they brought along "certain enchanters called Brahmans, who by incantations and diabolical arts could paralyze and control the fish." The men Marco Polo took for sorcerers were in fact Brahman priests, members of the highest caste in Hindu society.

Pearl oyster fishing ended in the nineteenth century, but if one sails through the string of rocky islets today, one comes across signs of the pearl divers. The Strait of Palk, more commonly known as Adam's bridge, is where the famous episode at the heart of the Ramayana

Two treasures of Pallava art in Mahabhallipuram, in the Indian state of Tamil Nadu :
the approach to the Ganges, the largest bas relief in the world (twenty-seven meters long and nine meters high)
and a temple on the bank, devoted to Shiva by king Narasimhavarmana II in the eighth century.

The elegant beauty
of the Dravidians ! The origin
of these dark-skinned peoples
has not been conclusively explained.
It is, however, certain that they were
engaged in trade with Babylon,
Tyr and Jerusalem as early as the
fourth century B.C.

took place. According to legend, the monkey devotee Hanuman constructed a bridge over the water to allow Rama, the god, to free his beautiful wife Sita, who had been abducted by Rawana, the giant king of Sri Lanka. Today Hindus still believe that the rocks that barely break the surface of the water are the vestiges of the bridge. They are, in fact, the remains of the isthmus that, until the end of the Quaternary era, linked Sri Lanka to India .
Contemporary life is far from being so poetic. The entire region is prey to permanent political instability, due to the terrible ethnic and religious war between the Tamils of the Jaffna peninsula and the Sri Lankan army. In the end of the 1980's India tried to interfere and the experience was disastrous. Indian Tamils joined the revolt and in 1991 assassinated the Prime Minister, Rajiv Gandhi.

*The small craft from southern India are often quite primitive.
They are made of pieces of wood that are tied together and later separated
to dry on the beach after being used for fishing.*

235

Tamil Nadu is primarily an agricultural region.
It is the only place left in India where a visitor can see
collective fishing on the river and elephants at work.

A pachyderm bathing at the end of the day is an unforgettable sight!

▷

The lives of this young *adivasi*, outcaste, and these Brahmans, members of the highest caste, bathing in a holy pool, are worlds apart.

The Province of Lar and the Kingdom of Tana

FROM SOUTHERN INDIA TO MAHARASHTRA

Despite an understandable lack of precision, Marco Polo carefully recorded his observations about Hindu society. He noted that its organization was pyramidal and profoundly inequitable. The social, political and religious system he was discovering had already existed for nearly three thousand years and remains the basis of modern Indian society today.

HINDU SOCIETY

The king was served by "barons who rode with him and are very important [...] and have great authority throughout the kingdom." Below them were the merchants, then the common people. He then recorded the importance of the Brahman priests. Finally, he was most surprised by the groups of saintly men, practitioners of non-violence who inflicted upon themselves harsh penance. They lived on the fringe of society, but their opinions were highly respected. These exceptional people "are called ciugi and live for one hundred and fifty to two hundred years; and even then their bodily faculties are intact [...] this is said to be because of the great abstinence they practice concerning food and drink." Marco also met some *yogin* and *sadhu*, those aesthetes who renounce all worldly possessions to attain a state of purity.

*Vaishya, members of the third caste,
selling religious objects in the galleries of a temple in Tamil Nadu.*

*A Brahman priest studying and
meditating in the cool dark corridors
of the Sharangapani temple
devoted to Vishnu.*

Hindu society as presented in *Description of the World* is, in fact, a fairly accurate picture of that society today. Although it was officially abolished in the middle of this century, the caste system still governs relations between Indians. As for the *sadhu* and other *yogin*, they are a common sight in villages and along the roads.

Marco Polo's book also abounds in details concerning the mores and the customs of the time; some have disappeared, others remain. For example, the rule of the *satî*, which required a widow to throw herself onto her husband's funeral pyre, no longer exists. Yet, the ritual cremation of corpses, taboos concerning food, the importance of astrology and sooth-saying, the exclusive use of the right hand for noble tasks, the respect due to sacred cows, the daily veneration of idols in different shrines, the ancient dances, even the traditional bamboo *charpai* (bed) that Marco saw, remain part of the daily scenes that visitors may witness today.

According to tradition, corpses
must be burnt by outcaste untouchables
and after cremation, the ashes thrown
into the waters of a river.

The bath ritual is one of the holiest Hindu rituals.
All of the castes (here, some **kshatrya**, the second caste)
purify themselves in the waters of the river before praying to the gods.

The suburbs of the major cities house poverty-stricken populations who,
attracted by the promise of urban prosperity,
left the countryside to crowd into miserable shantytowns.

The fourth caste are the **shudra**,
mainly lowly workers and peasants.

A **lambadi** woman from Hampi. She belongs to an ethnic and cultural group of nomads
considered to be in the same category as outcastes.

THE HOLY CITY OF MADURAI

Following their route westward, the travelers next entered the "province of Lar, where the Brahmans are born." Marco is referring here to Madurai and its region in western Tamil Nadu. In the past it was called Madura and was believed to have been created from a drop of immortality that fell from the hair of the god Shiva. It was a great literary center during the first three centuries of the Christian era, and later became one of the holiest places in India. Known as the Benares of the south, twentieth century Madura houses hundreds of Hindu schools and shrines.

Daily street scenes from Madurai :
primary school teachers on their way to a temple with their pupils decked out in their finery;
also one of the many sacred elephants going for a stroll.

A general view of the city
taken atop the southern gopuram (tower)
of the temple of Minakshi-Sundareshvara.

Each year its temples attract millions of pilgrims. It is also the biggest Brahman center of southern India. The Brahmans, members of the highest Hindu caste, who Marco considered excellent merchants, amazed him, "because, not for anything in the world would they ever tell a lie [...] even if it were to die." In fact, the Venetian had just discovered one if the strict rules of the caste. He soon discovered others, such as the prohibition against eating meat and killing animals, the obligation to wash oneself several times a day and to abstain from any form of licentiousness and any excess. They could be distinguished from all other Indians by the fact that "all Brahmans carry a cord of cotton on their right shoulder."

The holy cord, the *brahmasutra*, is still the emblem of contemporary Brahmans, but it is also carried by the *kshatriya* and the *vaishya*, the two castes just below the Brahmans. It indicates the *dvija*, the "twice-born," that is, those who have already been reincarnated at least once

A young Tamil peasant
and his little sister looking their best
for a trip into town.

*At the foot of the southern **gopuram** is the holy pool of the Golden Lotus.*
It is claimed that at the epoch of the Sangama, books were thrown in the pool in order to prove their value:
only the books worth reading floated on the surface

The large offering room in the temple of Minakshi. Non-Hindus may not enter.
An impressive number of priests have given themselves up to the goddess's service.

In Madurai there are over three hundred temples of all sizes.
It is considered the holiest of southern Indian cities.

and have progressed along the way towards final salvation. Madurai is located in the middle of a large fertile plain where a minimum of two harvests are brought in annually. Many small farming villages, each with its own modest temple, are near-by. In the evening, the faithful come to give homage to the gods. Tradition is stronger here than elsewhere. For Indians as well as foreigners the visit to Madurai is one of the highlights of a trip to southern India.

Southern India enjoys a tropical climate
that fosters luxuriant vegetation and biannual crops.

Every morning fishing boats with their famous
"shark sails" weather the headland of Cape Comorin,
the southernmost point of the Indian sub-continent.

CAPE COMORIN

The headland at the southernmost point of the Indian sub-continent is called Cape Comorin, the Comari of *Description of the World*. It was known to Ptolemy as Komaria Akron and is called Kanyakumari by the Indians. It is a particularly holy place for Hindus, who dedicated it to the goddess Durga. On a small rock facing the cape itself rises a shrine devoted to the Kumari, that is, "the Virgin," one of the attributes of Durga. Here, in this landscape of pristine beauty, the Sea of Oman, the Indian Ocean and the Bay of Bengal flow together. When there is a full moon, the setting sun and the rising moon will appear on the horizon at the same time.

The place is swarming with monkeys, which are considered holy and to which the faithful bring offerings and food. Already Marco Polo had been struck by the great variety of animals found here, particularly "monkeys, some of them of distinctive appearance and so large that you might take them for men."

One of the sights one must not miss is the early morning departure of the fishing boats putting out to sea. Reflecting the orange blushes of dawn, the light skiffs, crowned by a small triangular sail, in the shape of a shark's fin, shoot forward to attack the dark ocean.

THE MALABAR COAST

After rounding Cape Comorin, the Polo fleet undertook the northward voyage along the Melibar coast (present-day Malibar) of southwestern India. As the days passed, Marco noted the kingdoms of Quilon, Melibar and Ely. Without realizing it, he was describing the exact boundaries of the future state of Kerala, which corresponds closely to what was Malabar, the name that was given to the portion of the coast between the town of Mangalore and the river Ponnani. The large merchant ports of Calicut, Mahe and especially Cannanore, near which Marco Polo located Ely, all face out to the Sea of Oman.

Until the fifteenth century the region was populated by Muslims, Hindus, Christians and Jews. The former were famous for their strength and had build a powerful thalassocracy which dominated this part of the world. When Marco visited the country, "these wicked corsairs [...] (who) caused great losses to the merchants and those who sailed" were already beginning to lose ground to the inexorable rise of the Christians, today the second religion after the Hindus here.

Two village women in the Sabarimalai fields, proudly sporting their valuable nose-rings.

Backwaters *are typical of the Kerala coast. Networks of canals link the many coastal lagoons between Cochin and Quilon.*

*Cereal threshing during **kharif**, the first principal Indian farming season that lasts from May to mid-October.*

Marco Polo judged Melibar to be a "most great kingdom [...] (where) there is a great abundance of pepper and of ginger; likewise there is cinnamon in plenty and other spices, turbit which is a medicinal plant, and coconuts." The agricultural potential of Kerala was not lost upon the medieval traveler and has been confirmed over the course of the centuries. It is one of the richest farming provinces of the Indian Union.

Regular southwesterly rainfall, an abundant network of mountains and fertile soil make it possible to grow rice, spices, coconuts, fruit trees, and in the highlands, coffee and tea. The abundant forests of teak and hevea are also exploited.

The beach at Kovalam has the reputation of being " the queen of the southern Indian beaches."
Its renown is due to a micro-climate that preserves it from the bad weather of the monsoons;
the contour of the coastline keeps out high waves and strong ocean currents.

*The festival of Onam takes place
in September and October
and marks the end of the harvests.
Spectacular boat races around Kottayam
are part of the festivities.*

The architecture and decoration
of Hindu temples in Kerala
(here, those of Ettumanur and
Padmanabhapuram) are unique in India.
Their style results from the mixture
of Hindu subjects and ancient Dravidian cults.

THE REGION OF THANA

The long voyage to the north put the Polos in sight of the Maharashtra coast which is called "the great kingdom of Thana," in *Description of the World*. The name came from the ancient port of Thana, the capital of King Bimba around 1300. It is likely that Marco came through here in the year 1294. Today it is an uninteresting industrial town, thirty kilometers from Bombay, the second megalopolis of India, with thirteen million inhabitants.

A paddy harvest near Thekkady and village scenes in the region of Mandaggade in western Karnataka.
Over seventy per cent of the Indian population earns its living from agriculture.
The heart and soul of India is to be found in the country where ancestral ways of life prevail.

The western plains in the piedmont of the Dekkan plateau
are victims of periodic droughts.
Life is organized around the rivers that guarantee animal life as well as crop irrigation.

▷

One of the many ports of Bombay.
This urban center of twelve million inhabitants is now the second largest in India.
The old city was constructed on seven islands.
Its origin dates back to the second century and the Kuli,
a low caste specializing in trade and laundering; it is from them that the word coolie is derived.

Rabi is the main farming season in Gujarat.
Crops are sown in October and November and harvested from February to May.

The Kingdoms of Gozurat and Kesmacoran
FROM MAHARASHTRA TO MAKRAN

*White is the favorite color
of the Gujarati.*

$\mathcal{M}$*arco Polo's ships continued their route,
turning their bows further northwest. They left behind them the hot, humid coastal plain of Maharashtra.
In the background rose the eastern ghat, those high natural steps, covered in teak and palm tree forests, that set the limits
of the Deccan plateau. Soon, the low, flat lands of the "great kingdom of Gozurat" appeared.*

GUJURAT

It did not correspond to present-day state of Gujurat, which is much larger. Indeed, it consisted only of the Kathiawar peninsula and a few inland territories. It was increasingly threatened by the sultans of Delhi who wished to annex it. The Kathiawar peninsula, which is often called Saurashtra or "the region of the sun," based on the name of the great fifth century Rajput kingdom, is located between the marshy lands of Rann of Kutch and the Gulf of Khambhat known as Cambay to Marco Polo. It resembles a massive low platform covered with swamps and alluvial plains. This basalt hunk was once a large island cut off from Gujurat by an arm of sea that has now disappeared. Occasionally, low, isolated sand-covered crystalline massifs rise up, the highest attaining 1,117 meters. Clear forests grow near the summits. In one of them, the forest of Gir, some of the last surviving specimens of the Asian lion, now an endangered species, can be found.

JAINS

Marco Polo probably met Jains for the first time in Gujurat. Isolated amidst the Hindus and Muslims, they attempted to conserve their unusual faith. Their success is evident, as Gujurat is now home to more Jains than any other state. They are followers of the great master, Mahavira, a near contemporary of Buddha's. He established a religion which was in many respects similar to Buddhism, preaching non-violence and total respect for all forms of animal and vegetable life, since all have a soul. It is not rare to see a Jain walking along a road with the bottom of his face covered by a piece of material to avoid breathing in even one insect, or carrying a small broom to sweep away and avoid stepping on any living being, however tiny. Their philosophy keeps them from being farmers, an activity which destroys an entire chain of beings with a soul. The ultimate aim of a believer is to escape from the cycle of reincarnations and to be one with the permanent creation of the universe. Jainism is fundamentally atheistic, as is Buddhism, and is based on a very elaborate cosmological concept : the universe is eternal; it is represented by a standing man whose legs embody the lower world, whose body is the central world, where we live, and whose head is the upper world. Around him gravitate a triple envelope of air, vapor and ether. Beyond reigns an absolute void.

Palitana is one of the most important
Jain pilgrimage sites .
This fortress, built on twin hills,
includes nearly nine hundred temples
constructed since the tenth century.

The complex design of the gigantic temple of Adinatha in Ranakpur
symbolizes a **yantra** (symbolique representation of the universe).
It was built in the fifteenth century.

Jain temples (here, in Vimala Vasahi) hold statues of the **tirthankara**
or "river forders," saints responsible for guiding mankind along the difficult path
to reincarnation and purity.

Jain rituals are terribly complex.
Marriages take place during ceremonies that are more philosophical than religious.
As respect for life is their supreme duty, the faithful
and the temple servants wear pieces of cloth over their faces to avoid breathing
in any tiny insects or microbes, all living beings.

When Marco Polo sailed along the Pakistani coast he could never have imagined that one of the small villages would one day become the enormous port city of Karachi with a population of eight million people.

THE MAKRAN COAST

Following the coast, the Polos continued in a northwest direction. They left behind them a large, but unimportant, bay on whose shores there was a small fishing village. Several centuries later the southern Pakistani metropolis of Karachi would be founded here. The fleet then reached a region, called Kesmacoran in the *Book of Marvels*, that not only harbored a large merchant population, but was also infested with pirates. This was present-day Makran, Pakistan's maritime border that continues westward to Iranian Baluchistan. When the Polos passed through, the region was already politically unstable and served as a buffer zone between the Sultanate of Delhi and the Khans of Persia.
Geographically it is a compact, hostile set of mountains, with several summits rising over 2,000 meters. The Baluchi tribes have lived there for centuries, traditionally serving as mercenaries and smugglers. They sold their services to Indian princes and Persian lords for whom they would attack caravans on land and merchant convoys at sea. The lay of the coast, with its numerous coves and adjacent narrow valleys that plunge into the mountains, was conducive to this clandestine activity. Even today, Pakistani officials advise people not to visit this region alone. Even the capital, Kurbat, has kept a solid reputation for brigandage.

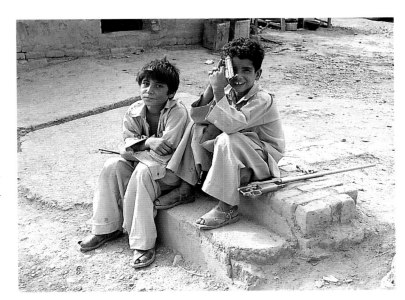

The entire Baluchi tribal area is a kind of free zone, uncontrolled either by Teheran or Islamabad. Smuggling is the main activity. The fierce, heavily armed mountain tribes are very touchy about their rights. The unusually conspicuous presence of central government authority will inevitably set off a bloody uprising. In these parts only tribal customary law has the authority to govern society, define common responsibilities and political orientations, and to raise taxes.

All along the 1,800 kilometers of the Omani coast, from the Persian Gulf to the Arabian Sea,
live peaceful fishing populations with modest incomes.

The Cities of Dufar, Calatu, Constantinople and Negrepont

FROM THE STRAITS OF HORMUZ TO THE MEDITERRANEAN

After leaving behind the dangerous Kesmacoran coast, the Polo expedition proceeded along a desolate shoreline towards the northwest. They entered the Straits of Hormuz where a multitude of Arab, Indian and Chinese boats plied the waters.

THE OMANI COAST

The modern visitor is likely to witness the same activity, except that now most of the vessels are warships. Their presence can be explained by the confusing political situation prevailing in the region. Iraq, Iran and the West are involved in a covert war of influence, after having let the canons speak until 1991.

At this point in his account, the author of *Description of the World* tells us that he went to the mysterious Male and Female Islands and even as far as Socotra, and from there on to Africa. Although it is certain that the Venetian never touched this continent, nor even got to Socotra, the possibility of his having reached the islands of Kuria Muria off the present-day Sultanate of Oman, to whom they belong, or of his having reached the southern coast of the

Sultanate, is remotely possible. Little seems to support this theory, but given the percentage of accurate information contained in *Description of the World* about the region, there remains a doubt. Some researchers believe that he simply gathered stories from sailors he met. Others think he quite likely did go at least to the Kuria Muria Islands, known as the Male and Female Islands during the Middle Ages. The following passage by Marco Polo seems to confirm that point of view : "And I am telling you that in this island fine quality ambergris is produced, because of the great number of whales that are caught in the sea." Indeed, the population on

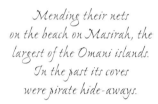

Mending their nets on the beach on Masirah, the largest of the Omani islands. In the past its coves were pirate hide-aways.

the southeastern coast of Oman and the Arabian Sea islands earned their living from whaling. However, the Venetian weakens his case with such stories as how the men went from their island to the women's island for love-making. If, however, one does accept Marco's claim to have visited these lands, one must then concede that he surely stopped at certain of the ports along the Omani coast. He may have visited the eastern part of present-day Dhofar, known then as Dufar, which has been famous for incense trading since ancient times. He claims to have been to Calatu, an ancient town located near present-day Sur, and he mentions the close political and economic relations it had with neighboring Persia. He may well have gone to see one of the many shipyards on the eastern Omani coast, for example at Agga, a tiny town facing the city of Sur. A modern visitor can still see there the construction of *dhows*, the famous Arab sailboats that sailors have admired since the tenth century. The passing of time has altered little : ancestral building techniques are the same and the workers seem to have stepped directly out of a history book.

A typical village on the eastern coast.
*The last of the **barrasti**, houses built*
of palm panels attached to wooden structures,
are giving way to stone
and concrete constructions.

*Agga, a market town near Sur, is one of the last places in Saudi Arabia where **dhows**,*
the famous Arabian sailboats are still made according to techniques unaltered since the Middle Ages.

*Most of the mud-walled Omani forts were built
between the sixteenth and eighteenth centuries.
Here, we see Birqat al Mawz
and the gates of the Jabrin fort.*

The basis of the sultanate is respect for tradition. An authentic continuity exists between the legacy of the past and the modern way of life.

Not far from Taqa, the mausoleum of one of the many Muslim saints
who came to meditate in the Samhan mountains throughout the ages.

The tribes of Dhofar
*(here, women from the Bait Kathir tribe, their faces covered by a **burka**, tribal mask)*
lived in large circular family homes. The straw roof is set on a stone foundation.
The last of these houses can still be found in the mountainous backcountry.

The **boswellia** is a small shrub
that grows only in Dhofar and Abyssinia.
During ancient times its resin provided incense
that was exported to the great temples of the Middle East.
Today it is used in the production
of the most expensive perfume in the world, Amouage.

An inhabitant of Mughsail.
The dark pigmentation of the Dhofari
is the result of inter-marriage
between Arabs and former black slaves
brought in from Zanzibar and Mombasa,
two seventeenth and eighteenth century Omani possessions.

The monsoons affect Dhofar from June
until September when the dried up rivers come to life
and the valley bottoms turn green,
allowing the herds to descend from the highlands to new pastures.

From Bandar Abbas to Venice

As the Omani coast dropped out of sight, Persia appeared on the horizon. Hormuz at last ! The mission that Kubilai Khan had entrusted to them was drawing to an end. The hazards of the voyage, storms, pirates and disease had all taken their toll. Over half of the fourteen junks that had left the port of Caiton had sunk, only eighteen of the original six hundred sailors had survived, and only one of Arghun's three dignitaries was still alive. The three Polos and Princess Kokachin, on the other hand, were all in good health.

Still, things did not take place quite as had been planned. Arghun died while the Khan's vessels were sailing towards Persia. His brother, Kaikhatu, had become the sovereign and when he saw the beautiful Kokachin, he decided to take her for his wife. Although the *Book of Marvels* does not say so explicitly, Marco Polo and the young woman seem to have become friends, if not lovers. Both of them were to suffer from the inevitable separation.

Laden with gifts from Kubilai Khan and from Kaikhatu, the three Polos set off on the route they had taken to the East, but this time in the opposite direction. Arriving in north-western Iran they intended to take the most direct route, by boat from Acre to Venice. The Muslims, however, had taken advantage of the bloody rivalries existing between the Christian communities of the Middle East to seize the city. As the overseas kingdoms no longer existed, the Polos had no choice but to go farther north. They thus set out for Trebizonde (present-day Trabzon) where they surrendered part of their riches to the Great Commène, as the Greek ruler liked to be called. Completely disgusted, the three travelers finally reached Constantinople.

Once again *Description of the World* is very succinct. From other sources, however, we learn that a certain Mabilia or Manibilia Polo, a cousin of the elder Polos, lived in the Byzantine capital, and so they must have stayed with her. Marco succumbed to the charm of the city, despite the destruction resulting from the sack of 1204-1205. They soon bid farewell to Constantinople and embarked on a ship for Chalkis, the capital of Negrepont, as the island of Euboea was called during the Middle Ages. At the time, this island was one of the Venetian outposts in the western Mediterranean, lying conveniently close to continental Greece. It was a stop-over for many of the convoys en route to the Middle East. The three Polos stayed there briefly, then sailed on towards northern Italy, taking with them "many riches and much company," and, according to Marco Polo, "finally arrived safe and sound in Venice. This was in the year of our Lord 1295." Thus ended their return trip that had lasted three years.

They had left their native land twenty-four years earlier.

Their welcome in Venice

Description of the World does not tell us about the fate of the three travelers on their return to Venice. We have been able to learn what became of them from various other sources. According to legend, immediately after disembarking, they went to the family home and knocked on the door. A servant answered, inquiring who they were, to which they replied "the masters !" It sounds too good to be true. Even if the welcome was a warm one, one must not forget how many years had passed since their departure. Fiordelise, Niccolo's second wife, had been waiting for her husband for twenty-four years. She had borne him a son, conceived during his brief stay in Venice in 1271; he was now twenty-three years old. Marco made the acquaintance of his half-brother Maffeo, and perhaps his two other half-brothers, Zanino and Stefanino, whom his father is believed to have had with a certain Maria. Marco the Elder must certainly have been present and presided over this great family reunion.

We know very little as to the welcome they received from the authorities and the Venetian

Küçük Aya Sofia is the contemporary name for the Byzantine basilica of Saint Sophia.
It was built in the sixth century during the reign of emperor Justinian
and was transformed into a mosque in the sixteenth century by order of sultan Beyazit II.

Midday prayer in the great mosque of Sultan
Ahmet Camii, known as the "blue mosque."
It was built between 1609 and 1616
and until the nineteenth century was the starting
point for caravans heading to the Mecca.

population. There are two conflicting hypotheses. One, although rather unlikely, maintains that they were ignored by their fellow citizens. The other, based on official documents , indicates that they received a rather cool reception; the stories of the far-away lands they had visited smacked of heresy to honest Christians. And then, the Venetian population had other worries : the war with Genoa was at it height.

OPPOSITION BETWEEN THE GENOVESE AND THE VENETIANS

The animosity between Genoa and Venice dated back two centuries. They were rivals in every field : trade, culture, the army, the navy and art. They had never stopped fighting on land and on sea, resorting to the worst diplomatic stratagems and did not hesitate to ally themselves with dictators if they were enemies of their rival. This policy, of course, turned out to be disastrous for both cities. Therefore, in 1270 they signed a peace treaty in Cremona. Peace reigned when the Polos set out a year later.

While they were traveling in Asia, however, hostilities between Genoa and Venice were beginning again in a covert manner. The Genovese had become friendly with the Mongols, who were on bad terms with the Venetians. The latter signed agreements with the Muslim Mamelukes, who were fighting the Genovese. A veritable shadow war was in progress, punctuated by treason and intrigues. Mongol support had become a major stake in the conflict. Noghai, one of Genghis Khan's great grandsons, had allied himself with the Venetians in 1291. In 1294 Toktai, the new Khan of the Golden Horde, denounced the agreement and attacked Noghai. The Genovese took their side immediately, while the Venetians adopted a lower profile.

This masked opposition degenerated into open war between the two Italian cities in 1294, just before the Polos returned. A Genovese squadron annihilated part of the Venetian flotilla anchored in the port of Ayas. Reprisal was immediate. The Venetians attacked all the counting houses and convoys of its rival and declared a general mobilization. Marco Polo had hardly recovered from his voyage when he reluctantly found himself involved in the war as commander of a galley. Unfortunately, his ship was destroyed and he was taken prisoner. Once again there are two conflicting versions of this story. Some Venetian authors say he was captured with other commanders of Venetian vessels not far from the port of Ayas in 1296. Others claim he was taken prisoner after a heroic fight during the battle of Curzola in 1298. In either case, Marco Polo was a prisoner of the Genovese.

RUSTICHELLO OF PISA

Marco Polo may simply have been held hostage and was not a veritable prisoner. During his detention he made the acquaintance of a certain Rusta, nicknamed Rustichello, who was from Pisa and had been in Genovese jails for over ten years. He was an outstanding court writer and had already written several important literary works, in particular novels about the legends of King Arthur and the knights of the round table and Tristan. He had been in the employ of Kings Henry III and Edward I of England, among other sovereigns. Listening to Marco Polo give a detailed account of his adventuresome life, he offered to put them to paper. And Marco accepted. To avoid mistakes in the narration, Marco sent off to his father in Venice for the documents and notes he had taken during his long tour. This collaboration is the basis for the text known as *Description of the World*. The manuscript was finished in 1299, the same year that Genoa and Venice signed a new truce. The prisoners were all freed and Marco returned to Venice. It was after that that all of Europe learned about his incredible adventure.

THE DESTINY OF *DESCRIPTION OF THE WORLD*

The book was an exceptional success. It was received with as much favor among Marco Polo's admirers, as it was with criticism by his detractors. It is believed that the first version was written in French and others, in Latin, Toscan, Venetian, Pisan and Genovese; Spanish, German, Bohemian and Irish came later. One hundred and forty-three manuscripts are known to have circulated throughout Europe for one hundred and eighty years. It was only in 1477, twenty odd years after the invention of printing by Gutenberg, that the first printed copies appeared. The craze for the book continued to grow. Today, everyone has heard of Marco Polo. The accounts of the travels of Marco Polo, his father Niccolo and his uncle Maffeo have been published with several titles. The first was *Description of the World*, then came the *Book of Marvels* and finally, *The Travels of Marco Polo*. The Italian versions were entitled *Il Milione*.

MARCO POLO, "THE NOBLE CITIZEN OF VENICE."

Much has been written about the meaning of the term "milione." Some historians believe it is an allusion to the fabulous wealth the Polos were thought to have brought back with them from their travels. Others feel that it follows from Marco's the enumeration of the incredible treasures in the Great Khan's court and in the eastern kingdoms Still others discern a touch of Venetian mockery directed at their illustrious fellow citizen whom they suspected of embellishing the truth. How could people of the thirteenth century even conceive of a black oil (petroleum) that gushed from the earth and burnt continuously in Georgia? Or that "salamander" (asbestos) came from a stone and not from an animal? Or that the Great Khan had five hundred wives and twelve thousand barons? It was just overwhelming! Marco had committed the mistake of being ahead of his time. Nevertheless, he became extremely famous and was known by the Latinized name of "nobilis vir Marcus Paulo Milion," which he passed down to his descendants. The Italian nobility, and the Venetian nobility in particular, as well as most of the European courts recognized the importance of his book and judged the information as trustworthy. King Charles V insisted on owning three original manuscript copies. Even the Catholic Church, after its early reticence, condescended to recognize the authenticity of Marco Polo's account. A Dominican, friar Pipino, was delegated to meet Messer Milion and to translate the book into Latin so that it could be used to propagate the Catholic faith. Pipino found Marco to be "a wise devout gentleman, with honest morals" and he translated the book with unstinting zealousness. This official recognition granted by the pontifical throne was to guarantee *Description of the World*'s its international reputation. Marco Polo married a Venetian noblewoman, a certain Donata from the house of the Badoers. His wife's dowry plus his own personal fortune afforded the couple an extremely comfortable lifestyle. From then on the indefatigable traveler was content to live off his income; he never again left Venice. His wife bore him three daughters, Fantina, Bellela and Moreta. He passed away peacefully in 1324 at his home in San Giovanni Grisostomo. Nothing remains of Marco Polo besides a few manuscripts. His house burnt down in the 1596 fire in his neighborhood. His bodily remains were lost in 1806 when the royal Italian administration established by Napoleon destroyed the church of San Lorenzo and the chapel of San Sebastiano where he lay alongside his father Niccolo and his uncle Maffeo.

The seeds he sowed, however, were to grow quickly. In 1426 two copies of his work were brought to the court in Lisbon and gave the Portuguese captains the idea of following the African coast to reach Persia, India, Melaka, the Sunda Islands and finally China by sea. In 1480, a Genovese acquired two other copies. He was fascinated by Marco Polo's account and decided to reach Cipungu (present-day Japan) and India by the western sea, that is, the Atlantic Ocean. And in so doing, Christopher Columbus discovered the New World in 1492.

Conclusion

The adventures of Marco Polo stimulated relations between the East and the West during the Middle Ages. The Mongol sovereigns adamantly continued to request that the European popes send them missionaries. Thus, several delegations set out for China. The most successful was that of Jean of Montecorvino, a Franciscan sent by Pope Nicolas IV in 1289. In light of the numerous conversions obtained by Jean, the pope appointed him archbishop of Peking and sent along six new bishops. When Jean of Montecorvino died in 1330 the Great Khan, Rinchen Pal, and his successor, Toghan Temur, requested a replacement. In 1342 four papal legates led by Jean of Marignolli, reached the court of the Mongol emperor. This, however, was to be the end of the privileged relations between China and the West.

In the middle of the fourteenth century two important events took place that radically altered the situation. First, a great epidemic of plague devastated Europe between 1344 and 1348, drastically reducing caravan trade. In Persia and China, the Mongol authority was declining rapidly, which led to the rise in power of smaller Chinese principalities. The anarchic situation that resulted from the numerous uprisings against the Tartars finally brought to power a new Chinese dynasty, the Mings, founded in 1368 by Zhu Yuan Zhang. Paradoxically, for China this was a period of domestic prosperity and withdrawal from international relations. The empire was closed to foreigners for two centuries. The various overland routes permanently lost precedence to the maritime routes.

To be sure, a few caravans continued to follow the different portions of the Silk Route. Some European governments, Portugal in particular, sent ambassadors to the Far East. But the era of the great caravan routes was for all intents and purposes over.

The superb cities and the monasteries and temples with their works of art that marked the length of the old overland trails passed into disuse for many centuries and eventually disappeared. By the nineteenth century the Silk Route had been completely forgotten and accounts like those of Marco Polo were believed to be pure fantasy.

At the end of the last century, however, certain ancient vestiges were being rediscovered, almost by accident. First, travelers passing through, grave robbers and treasure hunters uncovered lost cities hidden by the sands; they were followed by scientists from all over the world who were attracted by the discoveries. Historians, archeologists and linguists came in rapid succession to the newly revealed sites. The most well-known of these expeditions were those of the Swede, Sven Hedin, the Englishman, Aurel Stein, the German, Albert von le Coq and the Frenchman, Paul Pelliot.

Thus, six hundred years after the fabulous voyage of Marco Polo, people could once again see what the Venetian had seen, thus proving beyond any shadow of a doubt that he had not lied.

It is only fitting that Marco Polo himself provide the conclusion to this book. Here is the voice of that "noble citizen of Venice:" "There has never been a Christian, Saracen, pagan or Tartar or any race of man, who has known , seen and studied so many things in the various parts of the world and so many of its great wonders as this same Messer Marco Polo; none other has made so many voyages nor has had so many opportunities to see and understand [...] For this reason he was convinced that it would be a great pity if he did not lay down in writing all the great wonders he had seen and had heard as true, so that other people who have not seen and do not know them may learn them thanks to this book."

The basilica of Santa Maria de la Salute
seen from the Grand Canal in Venice.
Construction began in 1631
and many changes were made,
until it was immortalized
during the eighteenth century
by seascape artists such as Canaletto.

Conception Graphic realisation
© BOWER
3 place aux huiles - 13001 Marseille

Photocomposition, execution and cartography
© PLEIN FORMAT
72 boulevard Notre Dame - 13006 Marseille

Photogravure
CITIEMME
corso Svizzera, 185 - Turin

Impression
EGEDSA
Rois de Corella,12, 16, Nave 1
08205 Sabadell /Barcelone)

© 1997 VILO -
25 rue Ginoux - 75015 Paris

The quotations from *Description of the World*
are taken from the unabridged text by A.C. Moule and P. Pelliot,
translated into French by L. Hambis with notes by S. Yerasimos
Published by © La Découverte, 1980, Paris